HOCKEY FIRSTS

**Inventions, Innovations,
Records & Milestones**

J. Alexander Poulton

OVER
TIME
BOOKS

The Publisher: OverTime Books is an imprint of Éditions de la Montagne Verte

Website: www.overtimebooks.com

Library and Archives Canada Cataloguing in Publication
Poulton, J. Alexander (Jay Alexander), 1977–
    Hockey firsts: Inventions, Innovations, Records & Milestones / J. Alexander Poulton.

Includes bibliographical references.

ISBN 978-1-897277-43-0

    1. National Hockey League—Miscellanea. 2. Hockey—Miscellanea. I. Title.

GV847.8.N3P688 2009   796.962'64   C2009-902515-9

Project Director: J. Alexander Poulton
Editor: Heather MacDonald
Cover Design: Joy Dirto
Cover Image: Images courtesy of © Minas Panagiotakis, #5273271 | iStockphoto.com; © Minas Panagiotakis, #4736607 | iStockphoto.com

We acknowledge the financial support of the Government of Canada through the Book Publishing Industry Development Program (BPIDP) for our publishing activities.

Canadian Heritage   Patrimoine canadien

PC: 1

Dedication

To the first time I saw a game at the Montréal Forum with my dad.

–J. Alexander Poulton

Contents

Introduction

It is obvious that someone is the first to do something in every aspect of life and not just sports, but when I began looking into who were the first to do things in hockey I found quite a few surprises. While there are some easy ones to figure out like who won the first Stanley Cup or who was the first to score 200 points during the regular season, many required a little more in-depth research into the origins of the sport. To illustrate the difficulty, take for example, the first game of hockey ever played.

Hockey, like most other sports, did not just spring up overnight and there is a great and ongoing debate as to the birthplace of the sport. So trying to find out where the first actual game was played is definitely a subject for some dispute and concern before making an informed decision to write about it. The choice came down to historical evidence, thus giving it the right to be called the "first official hockey game". The distinction goes to a game that was played on Montréal's McGill University campus in 1875. It holds the official title because of the written evidence of the game left behind and the fact that both teams were playing under a set of rules written down prior to the game.

In the course of my research I also came upon a few other gems that many might have never considered to be firsts, like the first riot caused by hockey or, as it is most commonly referred, the Richard Riot. If any fans were going to riot first it was going to be Montréal Canadiens fans. Canadiens fans already loved their team but they adored their superstar Maurice Richard. He was the focal point of the team and a saint to legions of devoted followers. And so in March of 1955 when he received a suspension from the league for fighting and hitting a referee, the people of Montréal went berserk. Lasting almost the entire night, Canadiens fans destroyed over a hundred thousand dollars in property and several arrests were made. Quiet was only restored after Maurice Richard went on radio and appealed for calm. There have been many hockey riots since that day, most notably in Stanley Cup winning cities.

I also found a few interesting stories that classify as firsts and will most likely never happen in the NHL again, like the story of an NHL head coach playing in goal for his team during a Stanley Cup finals game. The story of Lester Patrick, head coach of the New York Rangers, coming off the bench and playing in game two of the 1928 Stanley Cup finals against the Montréal Maroons is so strange and so improbable that it will never occur again.

There is also the odd story of Canada's first ever Olympic gold medal in hockey. Although the Winter Games did not officially begin until 1924, Canada is credited with having won its first gold medal in ice hockey at the 1920 Summer Games in Belgium! The Canadian team was invited to the games by the International Olympic Committee in the hopes that displaying a variety of winter sports to the world would make it easier to market a new Winter Olympics. The Canadian team went on to win the gold medal and were presented with an official paper stating that they had just won the first Olympic Winter hockey gold, but when the 1924 official Winter Olympics came along the 1920 gold medal was not deemed legitimate, only years later were the medals recognized and given official status; but the catch is that the 1920 hockey gold medal is registered under the Summer Games and not in the Winter.

This is just a sample of some of the hockey firsts that I have collected in the following pages. Obviously I could not get all the first facts into this book but I feel I have compiled the most interesting and fun to read stories from hockey's long history. I also must say that all firsts in hockey continue to be made and that I look forward to seeing what all the talented players have in store for us fans. Enjoy!

Chapter One

Firsts in the Game of Hockey

The First People to Play Hockey

Canadians will universally claim that hockey was born in their country. After all it was in Canada where the sport grew, and it is where the sport has attained a religious-like following. Personally insult Canadians and they will probably turn the other cheek, but insult their hockey, and you'd better watch out.

But as attached as Canadians are to their game, the origins of the sport can be traced back to places and countries that are sure to make Don Cherry shiver.

It is very difficult to pinpoint the exact time and place that hockey began, or any sport for that matter, because most often the development of a game acts more like an evolution. In the early 1700s, Dutch painters depicted people skating on a frozen lake, wearing skates, carrying sticks and chasing after some sort of ball. Now it might be tempting to claim that as proof of the birth of hockey but the game they were playing does not resemble the one we see today under the bright lights of NHL arenas. The English played a game a little closer to hockey called bandy, but it was played on a much larger surface, and while they used similar equipment, it still did not look like today's game.

What most likely occurred was that European settlers brought games similar to hockey from Europe, and once in North America a new game began to evolve out of the old ones. Halifax has the most historical evidence to support the claim that hockey began in their city. Through letters, eyewitness accounts and newspapers articles, the evidence showed that a game called hockey was played some time in the early 1800s in and around Halifax.

The earliest game in which two teams played under an agreed set of rules occurred during a game in Montréal on March 3, 1875. The game was played on the campus of McGill University and was organized by Halifax native James Creighton. Ever since that game in Montréal, hockey has exploded into an international phenomenon. But no matter how big or far the game spreads, its roots and its most devoted fans are and will forever be Canadian.

The Strange Birth of the Hockey Puck

It is hard to imagine hockey without the puck, but long ago during the game's first few steps, players tried everything but a vulcanized rubber puck to smack around the ice. Hockey requires that the object that's put into the net is able to resist the extreme cold temperatures and endure the constant smacking and slapping by all the players. A plethora of materials was tried before the miraculous discovery of the rubber puck.

As hockey grew in popularity across North America, players could not simply go to their local sports store and pick up a puck for a few dollars. They were forced to improvise with all kinds of things, from wooden discs cut out of local trees to frozen horse droppings, affectionately known as horse apples. Suffice it to say that the frozen horse apples were rarely used and had a tendency to come apart in players' faces when slapped too hard. The most common early form of the puck was the wooden disc. Usually cut from local hardwood, the wooden puck was a noble effort but it could not withstand the abuse by players and was too light to get off any good shots. So as the game grew, there was an increasing need for a "disc" that could stand up to the kind of play that was evolving with the sport.

Players found the most adequate substitute for the traditional wooden disc was a rubber lacrosse ball. It had the necessary weight for players to be able to take proper shots and could take repeated abuse from the hacking of the hockey sticks. There was just one drawback. It bounced around like a superball. This was especially problematic when hockey first moved indoors. Just ask any rink superintendent from the time.

Montréal's Victoria Skating Rink was the premiere indoor arena of the time. It was the centre of the Montréal's social and sporting life during the winter months. In the 1860s, the building was adorned with large beautiful windows to allow as much possible natural light into the arena because the electric light was still over ten years away.

The big windows provided plenty of light and aesthetic beauty, but also plenty of opportunity for disaster. During one especially heated game, the players whacked at the ball with little care for any of the windows close by. Some low wooden boards had been set up to protect the onlookers but in the heat of the match, it became almost impossible to control the bouncing ball. It was just a matter of time before the ball cleared the low boards and smashed right through the arena's windows. After this occurred several times, a frustrated rink manager grabbed the ball, took a sharp knife and cut off the top and bottom sections, leaving only the flat middle section for the players to use. The players, annoyed at first at having their ball cut to pieces, noticed that the new flat "puck" slid along the ice easily, still provided the resistance they needed, and most importantly, didn't smash any more windows.

The rubber puck was later invented in 1872.

The First Fox Glow Puck

In the history of the game there have been many adjustments to the rules and equipment to ensure that the product on the ice remains entertaining and relevant with the changing times, but not all ideas and changes have been good ones.

There are many in hockey circles that are opposed to any changes to the game, but even with all the developments over the years, the game has remained basically the same: five players with sticks chasing a rubber puck. Players' salaries might have skyrocketed, the number of teams tripled, and most people were now watching hockey games from the comfort of their own homes, but the game remains close to its roots. For Canadian hockey fans, this emphasis on tradition has kept them linked to the past even as they looked forward in their pursuit to perfect the game. Each and every change is looked at with a fine-tooth comb and is not implemented without much debate. One of the strangest changes was, most certainly, the glow puck, better known as the FoxTrax puck.

In the early 1990s when the NHL expanded into non-traditional markets like San Jose and Tampa Bay, they were faced with educating a fan base that was unfamiliar with the many aspects of the game. While there were a significant number of fans willing to embrace the game, the NHL thought that they could use some help in following the action on the ice.

To help the NHL reach a wider audience, Fox network was contracted in 1994 to broadcast games in the United States. However, after one full season, the network was getting constant complaints from its audience. The fans liked the fights and the fast-paced action, but a large majority found it difficult to follow the tiny black puck on their TV screens. The Fox network responded to these complaints, with the approval of the NHL, and created the FoxTrax puck to remedy the problem.

The FoxTrax puck was simply a regular NHL puck that was cut in half and had a tiny circuit board inside, attached to a shock sensor and infrared sensors. The two halves were then sealed, and the puck, with the same weight, balance and rebound as a regular puck, was ready for action. The batteries that powered the puck were designed to last for around 30 minutes but often it ended up being just 10 minutes. All this technology inside the puck was placed there for the simple reason so that people sitting at home on their couches could follow the puck.

The infrared sensors would relay information back to the cameras that would then translate the pucks movements on screen into a bluish glow around the puck. When a player hit the puck, a bluish comet tail would light up onscreen indicating the puck's direction, and as an added feature, when the puck moved faster that 70 miles per hour, a red comet tail appeared to obviously indicate that the puck was going fast.

Reactions to the puck were mixed. American audiences welcomed the addition with open arms. A survey of the American public's reaction found that an overwhelming majority appreciated the extra help in following the game. However, hockey purists (mostly Canadians) were not happy with the comet tails and bluish glow on their TV screens, and complained that the glowing puck made hockey look like a video game. The most common response was that it should not be that hard to follow a black puck on a sheet of white ice. NHL players even complained that despite all the measures taken to ensure that the new pucks matched the old in every way that the puck reacted differently on the ice.

Despite its detractors, the Fox Network kept the glow puck until the end of the 1998 Stanley Cup finals. The following season the U.S. NHL broadcast rights were handed over to ABC, and the glow puck died along with it. Hockey purists everywhere breathed a collective sigh of relief.

First Artificial Ice Rink

The first artificial ice surface was opened in Charing Cross in London, England in 1876. The ice surface was designed and constructed by a Professor Gamgee. The professor built the 100-square-foot surface over a network of copper pipes containing a mixture of glycerin and water that circulated through the pipes after being chilled by ether. The freezing cold pipes were then covered with water and the first ever artificial rink was born. Canada was slow to follow the British example, opening up their first artificial rinks in 1911 in Vancouver and Victoria, British Columbia. Built by Lester and Frank Patrick, the artificial rink was a necessity in BC's temperate climate, since natural ice rinks did not have a very long lifespan. One year later, Eastern Canada followed suit, and the first artificial rink opened in Toronto. By 1920 there were still only four artificial rinks in the whole of Canada.

The First Temple of Hockey (Montréal Forum)

While today on the site of the old Montréal Forum stands a movie theatre and a shopping mall complex, there once stood on the corner of Ste-Catherine and Atwater one of the greatest and most hallowed rinks in all of hockey.

The Forum played host to some of the greatest players in the history of the game and was the home of 24 Stanley Cup championship teams. Over the years the Montréal Forum has been associated with the exploits of the Montréal Canadiens. It would not be a mistake to do so since the team had many prosperous years under its rafters, but originally the Forum was built for a completely different team.

Montréal had long been culturally and economically divided along linguistic lines, and those divisions also extended into the realm of sports. When the National Hockey League opened for business, Montréal had two teams; the Canadiens represented the French in the city and the Wanderers the English. But when a fire destroyed the home arena of the Wanderers just a few games into the 1917-18 season, they could not afford to build a new arena, and Montréal lost its English hockey franchise.

But the wealthy elite Anglophones of the city would not be without a team for long. In 1924 a group of wealthy Montréal businessmen and politicians got together and decided that they would form a new Montréal team called the Maroons. But in order for them to be admitted to the league, they would have to build a new arena. A site on the corner of Ste-Catherine and Atwater was chosen, and in 159 days the Montréal Forum opened. Although it was constructed for the Maroons, the Montréal Canadiens played many "home" games in the Forum (the Mont-Royal Arena was their official home, but it soon proved to be too small and the team bounced between the Forum and Mont-Royal Arena before officially sharing it as their home with the Maroons in 1926), and on November 29, 1924, the Canadiens were the first to play on its ice surface when they beat the Toronto St. Pats 7-1 before a crowd of 9000 happy fans.

That first victory set off a tradition of winning under the Forum's floodlights that would extend through decades of triumphs, defeats and tragedies—all witnessed by a city that flocked to the gates of the Forum like pilgrims to church on a Sunday morning. Indeed it was under the roof of the Forum that hockey in the city of Montréal developed into a religion of its own. With its groups of devoted fans—some fanatical and others simple believers—all were united under one roof and eventually by one team.

The games in the Forum between the Maroons and the Canadiens were especially heated affairs, with the French rooting for Les Canadiens and the English for the Maroons. That animosity was carried onto the ice as well, always providing entertainment for crowd. Those were the days of players like the Canadiens' Howie Morenz, Georges Vezina, Aurel Joliat and Sylvio Mantha; and the Maroons' stars Nels Stewart, Babe Siebert, Clint Benedict and Alex Connell. But the Maroons would eventually fold, and the Forum was left to the Montréal Canadiens to watch over. The Canadiens proved to be good tenants, lending the Forum the glory that they carved out over the decades of championships and Stanley Cups. But the history of the Forum is not all rosy.

After the Canadiens lost hockey's "Babe Ruth," Howie Morenz, to a devastating on-ice accident, the Forum did not see another superstar in the city until Maurice Richard came along in 1943 and brought back an energy into the building that had left the moment Morenz had injured his leg. Under the leadership of Richard, the Forum played host to the greatest collection of players in the Canadiens history. Names like Moore, Lach, Blake, Harvey, Plante, Durnan and Bouchard were the heart of the team while Richard provided its soul. But it was during those glory years when one incident under the roof of the Forum marked the career of one player and gave voice to the frustrations of a city. It would come to be known as L'Affair Richard or The Richard Riot.

Still more than 50 years after the incident occurred, people still talk about the game in Boston where the Rocket and Bruins Hal Laycoe got into a stick-swinging match and when Richard then proceeded to pummel the Bruin and linesman Cliff Thompson in the process. Richard was subsequently suspended for the remainder of the season and the playoffs for the incident by league president Clarence Campbell. When Campbell showed up for a game at the Forum on March 17, 1955, fans could not contain their anger at the league president for having removed their hero from the game. At first Campbell was greeted with a chorus of boos, but it was soon followed by popcorn, beer and eventually a tear gas canister that sent thousands of angry fans out into the streets where they mixed with other angry fans outside and sparked a riot that left the streets of

Montréal in shambles. It was a dark day in hockey history but it only added to the mystique of the Montréal home of hockey.

Once hockey returned, the Forum hosted five straight Stanley Cups through the late '50s, and added to the total through the '60s, '70s, one in the '80s and one in the '90s.

Apart from hockey, the Forum played host to countless other events and spectacles that marked its long history—boxing matches, circuses, concerts, ice shows, the Harlem Globetrotters and some of wrestling's greatest shows. Sports media often dubbed the Forum as Montréal's shrine to hockey, but the building often served as a gathering place for a variety of religious groups over the decades as well. Presided over by Archbishop Paul-Emile Leger from 1950 to 1953, midnight mass was held at the Forum and attracted crowds of up to 14,000.

But as the years dragged on, it became more apparent that the Forum was beginning to show its age and that a newer arena with more seats and luxury boxes had to be constructed in order for the building to remain competitive. The Forum had already undergone several reconstructions, but for the modern NHL, the old site would have to be abandoned. It was a difficult decision to move the franchise from the hallowed ground of the corner of Ste-Catherine and Atwater to the downtown site on de la Gauchetière Street.

While the new building has all the modern amenities, it lacks the feeling, emotion and sense of history that one used to get when walking into the Forum. There will always be just one Montréal Forum.

First Female Hockey Game

While it will always be disputed as to when the first game between all-women teams was actually played, the first official recording of a game appeared in the *Ottawa Citizen* newspaper on February 11, 1891. Although the teams were not named, it was reported as an entertaining game in which the ladies played rather well. By 1894, regular women's games were popping up all around North America. In 1896, the Ottawa Citizen reported on one such women's game saying, "Both teams played grandly and surprised hundreds of the sterner sex who went to the match expecting to see many ludicrous scenes and have many good laughs. Indeed, before they were there very long, their sympathies and admiration had gone out to the teams. The men became wildly enthusiastic."

First All-Black Hockey League

While no black player could even entertain the hope of landing a regular spot in the National Hockey League or any other pro league until Willie O'Ree broke the NHL colour barrier in 1958, black hockey players could find a place in the Maritimes Coloured Hockey League. Formed in 1894 in Nova Scotia the league featured teams from across the Maritimes and lasted until 1930. The league was known for its fast action and high scoring. The games were played on an invitational basis, and competition was more for fun than for glory. The focus on family fun met a need in the region and kept the seats full for over two decades.

The players from across Nova Scotia, Prince Edward Island and New Brunswick took the game seriously and are an integral part of the history of the game. The league is often credited as being the first to allow the goaltender to fall to the ice to cover the puck. In all other leagues, if the goaltender's feet left the ice, a penalty was imposed. In fact, goaltenders were not even allowed to fall to the ice in the NHL until 1917.

One of the league's players has also been credited with a technique in hockey that has become the bread-and-butter of many modern day players such as Zdeno Chara and Sheldon Souray. When asked, most hockey fans might mention guys like Bernie "Boom Boom" Geoffrion, Bobby Hull or Frank "Bun" Cook as the first players to take a slapshot. But hockey historian George Fosty makes the claim that the originator of the infamous slapper was Eddie Martin of the Halifax Eurekas just over 100 years ago. Fosty discovered in the course of research for his book on the coloured hockey leagues, *Black Ice: The Lost History of the Coloured Hockey League 1895-1925*, newspaper articles and accounts of Eddie Martin terrorizing in the league with a powerful shot that made him one of the better players in the league. Fosty claimed that since most of the black hockey players played baseball in the summer months, that resulted in a style that led to Martin's slapshot.

"What we see in Nova Scotia is these isolated communities that grew up around white communities, and they just seemed to develop this unique brand of hockey," said Fosty in an interview with Canwest News Service.

First Pro League

For a long time it was believed that the International Hockey League, which formed in 1904, was the first ever fully professional league in the history of the game. The league, which was based out of Northern Michigan, had five teams and attracted a lot of the superstars of hockey. But another league out of the United States claims the prize as the first pro league. The Western Pennsylvania Hockey League (WPHL) started out as an amateur league in 1890 but made the switch to a fully pro league in 1902. Going professional meant the league was better organized and the players were fully paid. The WPHL folded just two seasons later before eventually returning in 1907.

The Birth of the NHL

Of all the hockey leagues that had sprang up and just as quickly failed in Canada and the United States in those first few humble years of professional and amateur hockey, the formation of the National Hockey League in 1917 was not taken very seriously. World attention was focused on the war raging in Europe, and the league had the problem of getting enough able-bodied and skilled players into the league since many were overseas fighting for their country. It was a risky venture, but it was backed up by some of the greatest business and hockey minds the game has ever seen.

With the folding of the National Hockey Association, the National Hockey League was formally established on November 26, 1917, led by President Frank Calder. They originally began the season with four teams, but when the Montréal Wanderers' arena burnt down, the team could not afford to rebuild and were forced to fold their team becoming a footnote in hockey history. The three remaining teams, Montréal Canadiens, Toronto St. Pats and the Ottawa Senators, finished off the season with the Toronto St. Pats coming out on top as the first Stanley Cup champions of the National Hockey League.

Despite the loss of the Wanderers and the lack of fit men, the NHL had firmly established itself as the premiere professional hockey league in North America. Fans began to flock to the games to see stars like the Canadiens' Phantom Joe Malone, who scored 44 goals in just 20 games, and Senators' goaltender Clint Benedict, who "accidentally" fell down so much making saves that the league changed the rules to allow goaltenders to use that strategy. Since the formation of the National Hockey League, the game has changed to meet the demands of its fans and players, but the passion for the game remains the same as when the first puck was dropped on December 19, 1917, at the first NHL game.

The First Stanley Cup Victory

By the 1880s hockey was exploding in popularity across Canada. From frozen ponds to well-kept skating rinks, hockey was quickly becoming the favourite pastime of Canadians whether they were watching the games or playing them. When Sir

Frederick Arthur Stanley, Baron Stanley of Preston, arrived in Canada to assume his duties as Governor General in 1888, he was quick to note the popularity of the game that was sweeping the nation and decided to create a trophy that would be awarded to the best team in the country annually. Lord Stanley wrote of his intentions in a letter to an aide after he had returned to England:

> *There does not appear to be any outward sign of the championship at present. Considering the interest that hockey matches now elicit and the importance of having the games fairly played under generally recognized rules, I am willing to give a cup that should be annually held by the winning club.*

Lord Stanley had a trophy made at a local London silversmith for about $50, and it was shipped off to Canada where two trustees were given the responsibility of picking the teams that would fight for the right to hold the Cup. At the end of the 1893 season, the Cup was awarded to the winners of the Amateur Hockey Association champions, the Montréal Amateur Athletic Association, without any other teams competing for the Cup in a playoff round. The first actual competition for the Cup took place one year later in 1894 when, at the end of the AHA regular season, three teams vied for possession of Lord Stanley's Cup. The first ever Stanley Cup playoff game was held on St. Patrick's Day between the Montréal Victorias and the Montréal AAA. The AAAs won the game by a score of 3-2, then went on to defeat a third challenger, the Ottawa Capitals, to win the Stanley Cup for the second year in a row.

As the popularity of hockey and the prestige of winning Lord Stanley's Cup grew with each passing year, more and more teams vied for the honour of being the champion of the country's newest and most popular sport. With this new-found interest in the game, certain players began to shine above others, and teams negotiated heavily with the best players in order to secure themselves the best chances at winning the Cup. Hockey fever was born, and it was here to stay.

First Year Stanley Cup not Awarded

Throughout World War I, soldiers had been fighting in trenches across Europe. Confined to cold trenches, fighting and sleeping in dirty water beside dead or dying soldiers and an army of rats, many soldiers began to develop what appeared to cold symptoms. As soldiers returned home from the war, an influenza virus began to spread among the populations of the world. Over 21 million people died throughout the world from the Spanish Influenza. In Canada and the United States, entire communities were wiped out. In an attempt to minimize the effect of the disease, government officials closed schools; large celebrations and family gatherings were discouraged; and sporting events were cancelled.

In only its second year, the National Hockey League faced a major roadblock to establishing itself in North America. The Spanish Influenza had begun to affect not only the players but also the large number of people who came to watch games. Attendance at the games had been significantly reduced by government warnings to avoid public gatherings. Banners were plastered all over the cities warning people how to avoid contracting the virus. There was an air of panic across the country as families and communities began to break up because of the number of cases that developed.

The players and teams in the NHL were not immune to the disease either. At the start of the 1918-19 season the NHL had only managed to sign up three teams to play for the season and a chance for the winner to play against the rival league of the Pacific Coast Hockey Association. The teams were the Ottawa Senators, the Montréal Canadiens and the Toronto Arenas. But halfway through the season, the Toronto Arenas withdrew from the league because of financial problems, and the league was forced to play a best of seven series between the remaining Senators and Canadiens with the winner to battle the Seattle Metropolitans, winner of the PCHA title.

Led by Newsy Lalonde, the Canadiens proved to be the winners as they easily beat the Senators four games to one. While preparing for their battle against Seattle, several Canadiens players fell ill. At first most thought it was the common cold, but the symptoms progressed, and by the time the final game (scheduled for April 1, 1919) came around several of the players had fallen seriously ill.

It was believed that the Canadiens players picked up the illness while in Seattle for their first game of the finals. Returning to Montréal, Newsy Lalonde, Joe Hall, Louis Berlinquette and owner George Kennedy fell ill with influenza, leaving Georges Vezina, Odie Cleghorn and Didier Pitre as the only players left healthy enough to skate. The Seattle team arrived in Montréal with seven players in the recovery stage of the virus, all in bed at the same time. Rumours began to spread among the sick players that it was because they had played so hard against the other teams to get to the finals that their bodies had weakened and become more susceptible to the disease.

With more and more players becoming violently ill from the epidemic, the decision came down from NHL management on April 1 (just before the start of the final game in the Stanley Cup playoffs) that the game would be cancelled, and because the series was tied, no winner would be declared. Four days after the decision to cancel the playoffs, Canadiens star "Bad Joe" Hall lost his life to the influenza virus in a Seattle hospital, proving that the league had done the right thing in cancelling the playoffs and potentially saving lives.

The First Canadian National Olympic Gold

It has gone down in the history books that Canada's first gold medal in Olympic ice hockey came at the first ever Winter Olympics in Chamonix, France, in 1924, but Canada technically won its first ever Olympic ice hockey gold at the 1920 Summer Olympics in Belgium.

The Winnipeg Falcons had just come off an incredible season in the Senior Amateur Hockey League, winning the Allan Cup Championship. After their display of superior hockey skills, they were asked by the International Olympic Committee (IOC) to join their fellow Canadian athletes at the 1920 Olympics in Antwerp, Belgium. It did seem a little strange that an ice hockey team was being invited to compete in the Summer Games, but they had also invited figure skaters to the Olympics, so it appeared that the IOC was pushing to open a new winter version of the Games.

With dreams of Olympic gold in their heads, the Canadian men's hockey team bulldozed their way through the competition beating the U.S., Sweden and Czechoslovakia by a combined score of 28-1.

Along with receiving their shiny new medals, the Canadian hockey team received an official certificate stating that they had indeed won the hockey gold medal of the first official Winter Olympic Games. The Winnipeg Falcons beamed with pride at the gold medals around their necks, knowing that they would go down history as winning in the first ever Winter Olympic Games. But years later, the IOC repealed their decision to name the 1920 Olympic Games as the first Winter Games and handed that honour to the 1924 Winter Olympics in Chamonix, France.

At those 1924 Olympics, the Canadian hockey team again won the gold medal and was officially recognized as the first team to win Olympic hockey gold. It was only until many years later that the 1920 Winnipeg Falcons were acknowledged as official Olympic champions, although for the 1920 Summer Games.

Foster Hewitt's First Broadcast

Starting off his career as a reporter with the *Toronto Star* in the early 1920s, Foster Hewitt's job was to broadcast Toronto symphony concerts on CFCA, the newspaper's radio station. On the day of March 23, 1923, his boss approached him and told him that his regular broadcast schedule had changed. That night he would have to report to Toronto's Mutual Street Arena and broadcast the playoff game between two local amateur teams. It was an assignment that all the senior broadcast staff had turned down, so it got dumped on the shoulders of the wet-behind-the-ears cub reporter.

Arriving at the Mutual Street Arena, Hewitt took up his spot in a small glass box close to ice level. Teetering on a wooden stool and occasionally wiping the fog off the glass to see the play, Hewitt spoke into a telephone that doubled as a microphone and gave his first ever play-by-play of a hockey game. The connection was scratchy and telephone operators constantly interrupted him, but Hewitt managed to get through the three periods. He did not know it at the time, but that 60-minute broadcast would change the history of the game for generations of hockey fans. "For 60 minutes I talked, sweated, and window cleaned. I couldn't wait for the game to end," said Hewitt.

Soon he would graduate to NHL broadcasts and become the most recognized voice of hockey across Canada. Every Saturday night, kids across Canada and the United States gathered around the radio to hear Hewitt's familiar greeting: "Hello Canada and hockey fans in the United States." With baited breath, they would wait and listen for the familiar Hewitt cadence, on the edge of their sofas as he described the play-by-play on the ice. "Barilko gets the puck. HE SHOOTS! HE SCORES!" During his time Foster Hewitt was the authoritative voice of hockey in Canada and that, in his own way, united Canadians from coast to coast. He thought hockey was so important to the identity of Canada as a country that when Canada took on the Soviets in the 1972 Summit Series, he came out of retirement to broadcast those games and in doing so left us with one of the most memorable moments in our history:

Cournoyer just touched it. Savard, getting it at centre ice, clearing it off a skate. It goes into the Canadian zone. Yakushev, a dangerous player, is belted on that play. Cournoyer rolled it out, Vasiliev going back to get it. There's 1:02 left in the game.

A cleared pass on the far side. Liapkin rolled one to Savard. Savard clears a pass to Stapleton. He cleared the open wings to Cournoyer. Here's a shot! Henderson made a wild stab for it and fell. Here's another shot, right in front... They score! Henderson has scored for Canada! And the fans and the team are going wild! Henderson, right in front of the Soviet goal with 34 seconds left in the game!

And it all began with one little broadcast in a steamy booth for an amateur hockey game.

Hockey Night in Canada is on the Air

On the night of October 11, 1952, in a game between the Montréal Canadiens and the Toronto Maple Leafs, people across Canada got their first taste of what would become a Saturday night tradition in homes across the nation with the first televised broadcast of the Canadian Broadcasting Corporation's *Hockey Night in Canada* telecast. A nation used to getting their hockey fix from the voice of Foster Hewitt over the radio could now watch their hockey heroes on the ice for the first time.

For over 50 years the *Hockey Night in Canada* formula has stayed pretty much the same in an era of 30 NHL teams, playoff games in June, and of course, the dreaded experiment with the glowing puck. Let's hope it continues to stay the same.

First Forward Pass

For years fans of modern hockey complained that there wasn't enough scoring in the game.

Through the late 1990s, teams began to play a defensive style of hockey that led to low-scoring games and increasingly low attendance. So the NHL changed the rules and have now opened up the game and increased the average goals per game. Now go back six decades, and the league was suffering from the same exact problems of the '90s.

Before 1929, goaltenders ruled the National Hockey League. In one season Montréal Canadiens goaltender Georges Hainsworth recorded 22 shutouts in 44 games. The name of the game was defence since forward passing in the offensive zone was not allowed, so it was extremely difficult to enter the opposing team's zone. Add to that the fact that teams were allowed to keep as many players as they wanted in the defensive zone while sending one or two men on an offensive rush in order to protect a lead. All this changed in 1929, when the league instituted a set of groundbreaking rules that would change the game forever.

To open up the game and increase the forward lagging stats, the NHL decided to allow forward passing and penalize a team that kept more than three players (including the goaltender) in the defensive zone while the play moved up the ice. The difference was immediate. Players' scoring

percentages skyrocketed as goaltenders' save percentages plummeted. Just a year earlier, Montréal
Canadiens star forward Howie Morenz was in
the top five of the regular scoring leaders with
17 goals in 42 games; the next year with the
new rules, Morenz's stats increased to 40 goals
in 44 games. Goaltenders stats also increased as
George Hainsworth's amazing 0.92 goal average
increased to 2.42 in just one season.

Chapter Two

Goaltending Firsts

First Goaltender to Weigh over 300 pounds without Gear

As a kid I had always wondered why teams never simply hired a morbidly obese man to stand in front of the net to block the puck. Sure it would take the sport out of the game, but it sure would be effective. The only goaltender to come close to covering the entire net was one Billy Nicholson. Playing professional hockey from 1901 to 1917 with various teams, mostly in the Toronto area, ol' Billy's weight shot up to as much as 300 pounds. At that size he was not quite large enough to cover the whole net and not in good enough shape to actually make a save. As it was against the rules to fall to the ice intentionally for a save, reporters at the time loved to joke that when Nicholson did fall down, he managed to crack the ice.

First Brother vs. Brother Goaltending Duel

The history of the National Hockey League has seen many instances of brothers playing on the same team and even competing against each other as forwards or defencemen, but never had there been two brothers pitted against each other as goaltenders until March 20, 1971, when Canadiens rookie goaltender Ken Dryden went up against his brother, Dave Dryden, of the Buffalo Sabres. But it was a match up that almost didn't happen.

Ken Dryden had just been called up to the Canadiens and had noted that there was an upcoming game against his brother, but Habs coach Al MacNeil told him that he probably would not get the start, opting instead for veteran Rogie Vachon. But all that changed when Rogie Vachon went down in the second period with an injury. When Vachon didn't get up, Dryden realized that he would be playing in only his third NHL game. For the first time probably since they were kids, the Dryden brothers played in a game against each other.

Ken Dryden admitted in his bestselling book *The Game* that he didn't like having his brother at the other end of the ice: "I didn't enjoy that game very much…Seeing Dave in the other goal was a distraction I didn't want or need." Although he never voiced it, Dave was probably feeling the same way at the other end as he let in the first shot on net on a 70-foot shot by Canadiens Jacques Lemaire.

Montréal won the game with a 5-2 victory, but fans were more interested in the brothers on the ice than the final score. When the final buzzer sounded, Dave Dryden waited patiently at centre ice for his little brother; they gave each other a big smile and shook hands to the delight of the cheering crowd.

First Female Goaltender in the NHL

It was just before the Tampa Bay Lightning's first season in the National Hockey League and general manager Phil Esposito decided to explore an intriguing and innovative possibility—allow a woman play in an NHL game.

Esposito knew exactly what he was doing when he signed Manon Rhéaume to a professional contract in August 1992 and so did everybody in the hockey world. She was athletic, hard working, approachable and attractive. Newspapers across North America decried her signing to a professional contract as a mere publicity stunt to build interest before the start of the Lightning's first season in the National Hockey League.

The ploy worked like a charm as Rhéaume's face was plastered over every newspaper; she was in demand for countless interviews; and she was on everyone's television set before she'd even stepped out on the ice.

Rhéaume's 15 minutes of fame came in an exhibition game against the St. Louis Blues in September 1992. A crowd of about 9000 gathered in their seats before the game while Rhéaume circled in her zone preparing herself for the game ahead. She was able to stop the first three shots that came her way but on a long-range shot from Jeff Brown one slipped by her. After shaking the initial nerves off, she let in only one more goal off Brendan Shanahan. As the buzzer sounded for the end of the period, the crowd gave Rhéaume a warm round of applause for her effort. The Québec City native finished the period having let in two goals on nine shots, not too bad considering that Wendell Young, the next Lightning goaltender in the net, let in two goals as well.

Publicity stunt or not, Manon Rhéaume accomplished something that had never been done before, and she did not bend before all the media pressure. She never did get the chance to play in a regular season game but was signed to a three-year contract with the Lightning's farm team.

First Goaltender to Wear a "Mask"

While Clint Benedict was the first National Hockey League player to wear a mask in the net and Jacques Plante was the first to institutionalize it, they were not the first hockey players to seek protection from flying frozen rubber. That distinction goes to a Ms. Elizabeth Graham, the net protector for the Queen's University women's hockey team during the 1927 season, who wore a fencing mask to protect herself from injury. Guarding the nets for Queen's Golden Gaels, Graham wanted some protection from flying sticks and deflected pucks, so she grabbed a fencing mask from the Queen's fencing locker room, thereby establishing one of hockey's most recognizable fashion statements.

First Goaltender to Wear a Mask in the NHL

Although Jacques Plante is widely credited with bringing the goalie mask to the NHL, in fact, almost 30 years earlier, another goaltender was the first to play in a professional game wearing a distinctive type of facial protection.

On January 7, 1930, the Montréal Maroons were playing their local rivals the Montréal Canadiens in a heated game. The Canadiens star player was the legendary Howie Morenz, and all night he was buzzing up and down the ice giving the

Maroons star goaltender Clint Benedict a hard time. But the veteran goaltender was up to the task and had made several spectacular saves in the game to keep the score close. But with each additional shot on goal, Benedict had to put his body into increasingly vulnerable positions to make a save. Into the third period, the Canadiens had taken clear control of the game led by the speedy Morenz, but they could get nothing by the veteran Benedict. Looking for a hole, on his next shot, Morenz let a vicious slapshot go from the top of the circle. The shot found its way through the crowd and hit a screened Benedict in the face breaking his nose and cheekbone. Benedict had broken his nose this way many times before, and this time he decided to fashion a crude leather face mask to protect his nose in case he got another shot in the face. The mask was nothing like Plante later constructed to protect his face from flying pucks and errant sticks. Benedict's padded leather mask covered from his brow line, down his nose and across the lower portion of his face with a hole cut for his mouth to allow him to breath. In the only known picture of the mask, Benedict looks like Anthony Hopkins' Dr. Hannibal Lecter in the *Silence of the Lambs* movie from the scene in which Dr. Lecter is bound and masked by police.

But Benedict's padded leather mask wasn't enough to protect him completely, especially from a pro-slapshot, and after he took yet another shot to the face again breaking his nose, he was forced to retire from the game for fear of sustaining permanent damage.

After Benedict hung up his mask and pads, no goalie donned a mask in the NHL until Jacques Plante came along and changed everything for good.

First Goaltender to Wear a Mask on a Regular Basis

Standing in the way of a piece of speeding frozen rubber with nothing to protect your face is considered a little crazy even now, but before Jacques Plante donned a mask, it was usual for a goaltender to wear nothing on his face but a determined look.

The first professional hockey player to wear a mask was Clint Benedict of the Montréal Maroons in 1930, after his nose was broken by a shot from Howie Morenz. However, he quickly disposed of his crude leather mask because it blocked his view of the ice. No other goaltender wore a mask regularly during games until Jacques Plante defied convention and the urging of his coach.

Goaltenders were made of tough stuff in the early days of the NHL. They often played every game of the season and did not have a backup goaltender to replace them if they were injured or having a bad game. They had to contend with players crashing into the net, sticks catching them in the face and speeding pucks. Not wearing a mask forced goaltenders into a more upright style of goaltending. Only the bravest or craziest of goaltenders would crouch low and expose their faces to speeding pucks. Terry Sawchuk, for example, was one of those low-crouching goaltenders. His face displayed the price he paid with more than 400 stitches during his career.

It was considered a sign of weakness for a goaltender to wear a mask. Even though Plante often wore a mask during practice, Canadiens coach Toe Blake, who didn't really get along with the eccentric Plante, forbade him to wear it during a regular game for fear Plante would be thought puck shy.

"If you wear it when the season starts and have a bad game, the fans will blame the mask and get on you," counselled Blake.

Plante had many reasons for insisting that he be allowed to wear a mask. In 1954, his right cheekbone was fractured during practice by a shot from teammate Bert Olmstead, sidelining him for five weeks. In 1955, Don Marshall sidelined him again for five weeks by breaking his left cheekbone and nose on a shot, again during practice. After those incidents, Plante started wearing a mask during practice but never took it into a game because it hampered his vision too much.

"I kept it on religiously in practices from then on," said Plante in Andy O'Brien's book *The Jacques Plante Story*, "wondering all the while about what kind of a mask would be practical for wearing in games."

It wasn't until 1958 that Bill Burchmore, a salesman from Fiberglass Canada Limited, approached Plante with a design that moulded to his face and allowed him to see without obstruction. The finished product was thin, padded and tough as steel. It looked rather scary as two eyes peered out through two holes in the pale flesh-coloured form. Coach Blake would not budge, however, and did not allow his goaltender to wear the mask during a game. Blake said he feared that Plante would not be able to see the puck, certain that he wouldn't be able to follow the play properly. Plus there was the convention in the NHL boys club that real men did not need to protect their faces. However on November 1, 1959, Blake was forced to change his mind.

On that night, the Canadiens were playing the New York Rangers. Rangers forward Andy Bathgate broke in from the left wing just a few minutes into the first period, got within five metres of the net and took a hard rising shot right into Plante's nose. The referee saw Plante go down and whistled the play dead. Plante lay on the ice, out cold from the pain, his blood slowly pooling on the ice around him. After he was taken off the ice and stitched up by the Rangers' physician, Jacques secretly smiled to himself because he now had an excuse to use his mask, and Blake could say nothing to stop him. Taking one look at his goaltender's broken and bloody face, Blake conceded defeat, "Wear your mask if you want, Jacques." The Canadiens won that game 3-1 and won the next 11 games. Plante won the argument with his coach.

Still some people were slow to get used to the idea of masked goaltenders. Arturo F. Gonzales wrote of Plante's appearance in an article published in *Modern Man Magazine* of 1960:

> *Crouched in the cage with the sun-white glare of hockey rink floodlights carving his artificial "face" into deeply shadowed eye sockets and a gaping hole of a "mouth," Plante looks like something out of a Hollywood horror film. And when he uncoils and catapults from his cage toward an opposing*

player...his image stirs butterflies in the stomach of his target.

Although just a tad over dramatized, the image is more than clear.

Modern players, like Bernie Geoffrion and Bobby Hull, with their hard shots, make the mask a necessity for modern goaltenders, but it took one person to stand up to convention to make history.

"Plante was the happiest guy in the rink that he got cut [in the nose]," said long-time Canadiens broadcaster Dick Irvin Jr. "Don't ever feel sorry for him because he was looking for the opportunity."

First Appearance of the Goalie Pad

Before the February 16, 1896 Stanley Cup match between the Montréal Victorias and the Winnipeg Victorias, Winnipeg goaltender George "Whitey" Merritt decided to change into some new equipment. The hundreds of fans gathered to watch the game were shocked to see that Merritt had put on a pair of cricket pads outside his trousers to protect his legs. While there are pictures of other goaltenders prior to Merritt wearing cricket pads, Merritt gets credit for the invention because he wore them in a big game, a Stanley Cup final.

Emil Kenesky created the first modern goalie pads in 1924, when he modified cricket pads by stuffing and widening them to 12 inches. The wider leather pads became popular with goaltenders, and another significant change in pad technology was not seen until Boston Bruins goaltender Rejean Lemelin wore the much lighter Aeroflex pads in the late 1980s.

The Invention of the First Trapper

In the early days of hockey when the men were tough (barely any padding and no helmets qualifies as pretty tough) and played simply for the love of the game, goaltenders dressed in a similar manner to forwards. They wore extra padding only around the chest and legs; the rest of the equipment was basically the same as a forward's gear. With face exposed, those pioneer goaltenders had to rely on quick reflexes and an instinct for the game in order to survive. The modern goaltender has all kinds of padding to protect him from that frozen rubber disc, but in the early days, goalies didn't even have a blocker or a trapper.

Goaltenders wore gloves that were almost identical to those of the forwards and defencemen. Some modified their gloves by adding some extra padding, but the gloves mainly served as protection and not as specialized equipment to catch pucks. All that changed however in 1947 when Chicago Black Hawks goaltender Emile "the Cat" Francis altered the game forever.

Throughout much of his career, Emile Francis had known that the gloves he was wearing game in game out were not good enough to do the job. After several years of putting up with the traditional equipment, Francis began experimenting in practice with a specially designed first baseman's mitt that had an extended protective wrapping on the wrist. After a few adjustments to his creation, Francis felt it was finally time to take his new glove into a real game.

Francis first used the glove—a trapper—in a game against the Detroit Red Wings. When Detroit head coach Jack Adams got one look at the goaltender's new equipment, he immediately protested to officials that the glove belonged on the baseball diamond and not in a game of hockey. The issue was brought before NHL president Clarence Campbell, and after some consideration, he approved the new innovation and it was written into the rulebook that a goaltender could now use a glove to "trap" the puck.

Able to change the rules on the trapper hand, Francis now focused his attention on the stick hand. Tired of taking shots off the hand and have them deflect into the net because of the small surface area of impact, Francis began taping a rectangular piece of sponge rubber to the outside of his glove hand, thus inventing what would eventually evolve into the modern-day blocker.

First Goaltender to Score a Goal

Anyone brave enough to stand in front of Billy Smith's net usually ended up with the bruises to prove it. A fierce competitor, Smith protected the front of his net like it was his own home. If a player got in his way, Smith was never afraid to let him know that he had to move. Most of the time, he performed his antics when the referee wasn't looking, but he was often caught and earned himself a record number of penalty minutes for a goaltender. Smith had a clear justification for his violent behaviour.

"A goaltender has to protect his crease," Smith said. "If they're going to come that close, I have to use any means to get them out of there. If I have to use my stick, I'll use my stick."

Smith got his shot at cracking an NHL line-up with the Los Angeles Kings, but he played only five games with the California hockey club before the New York Islanders claimed him in the expansion draft of 1972. His competitive spirit was needed during the first few years of the expansion team's existence. Billy Smith's aggressive competitiveness often brought him into conflict with opposing players, with the media, with his coaches and even with fellow players.

But everyone knew that when game time came around, he was the hardest on himself.

After their first few years languishing in the basement of the league, the Islanders finally put together a winning combination for the 1974-75 season, and Smith's goals against average (GAA) went from 4.16 in 1972-73 to 2.78 in 1974-75. The Islanders became a good team in the late '70s, but they lacked the experience to go far in the playoffs. But as time went on, the Islanders added players such as Bryan Trottier, Mike Bossy and Clark Gilles who brought the raw talent and experience the team needed to be a winning team during a time when the Montréal Canadiens, Boston Bruins and the Philadelphia Flyers dominated the league. The team's patience paid off, and by the end of the 1978-79 regular season, the New York Islanders were the best team in the league. After another early exit from the playoffs at the hands of the New York Rangers, the Islanders started off the new 1979-80 season with a great deal of promise.

Smith had a feeling that things were going to go well for the team when he became the first goaltender to be credited with scoring a goal. It was November 28, 1979, and the Islanders were playing the Colorado Rockies in Denver. The play in question came in the third period. The referee signalled a delayed penalty against the Islanders, and the Rockies pulled their goaltender for the extra attacker. The puck was shot into the Islanders zone, touching Smith's chest protector before being picked up by Rockies defenceman Rob Ramage who made a blind pass back to the position he had just left. The puck slowly travelled along the ice and into the Rockies empty net. As the last Islander to touch the puck, Billy Smith got the credit, making him the first goaltender in NHL history to "score" a goal.

First Goaltender to Score a "Real" Goal

Often compared to Billy Smith because of his aggressive temperament, Hextall wielded his stick with impunity. Often controversial and always fun to watch, Ron Hextall quickly became one of the greatest goaltenders of his time.

Hextall first came into the league with the Philadelphia Flyers for the 1986-87 season and quickly established himself as one of the best goaltenders. The league had never seen a goaltender that played like Hextall. Jacques Plante was known for wandering from the net to play the puck, but Hextall took it to a whole new level. Most goaltenders at the time simply left the net to stop the puck for their defencemen and occasionally made short passes with weak backhands.

Hextall did things differently. He used his stick like a defenceman or forward to start a play from his zone, making heads-up passes and even scoring a goal or two. His teammates even used to pass the puck back to Hextall, who acted almost as a third defenceman. Once his hands dropped into the shooter's position, Hextall could fire outlet passes, bounce the puck off the glass and even lob the puck to avoid an icing call.

When Ron Hextall entered the NHL, he proudly declared that one day he would score a goal. "I've worked on my shot a lot. I can hit the net from our zone. I've even practiced a bank shot. I'm just waiting for the right situation," said the confident young rookie. Just one year later, he achieved his dream of becoming the first goaltender to shoot a puck into the opposition's net.

On December 8, 1987, during a game against the Chicago Black Hawks, the Flyers were up by two goals with one minute remaining. The Hawks pulled their goalie in favour of the extra attacker. Then came the mistake Hextall had been waiting for. Hextall got the puck on a bad dump-in by the Hawks, dropped his hands into the shooting position, took one last look at the empty net and fired the puck down the ice into the open net. Scoring one goal wasn't enough for Hextall, who repeated his amazing feat the following year with another in the playoffs against the Washington Capitals.

"I don't mean to sound cocky," Hextall said after scoring his first goal. "But I knew it was just a matter of time before I flipped one in."

Other goalies have since scored—Martin Brodeur, Jose Theodore, Chris Osgood and Evgeni Nabakov.

First Goaltender to Finish the Season with a Goals Against Average of 1.00 percent

With several Stanley Cups and Vezina Trophies under his belt, Georges Hainsworth achieved legendary status when he had the season of his career when playing for the Canadiens in the 1928-29 NHL season. In 44 regular season games, the Montréal netminder allowed only 43 goals and registered 22 shutouts for the lowest in NHL history at 0.92%.

First Goaltender to Finish the Season under 1.00 percent Goals Against Average

George Hainsworth finished the 1928-29 NHL season with a record setting GAA of 0.92. That same year, the Montréal Canadiens goaltender recorded another record of 22 shutouts, but all that great goaltending could not save the Canadiens from getting eliminated in the first round of the playoffs by the Boston Bruins.

First Goaltender Selected First Overall in NHL Draft

Michel Plasse was selected number one overall in the 1968 NHL Amateur Entry Draft by the Montréal Canadiens. Although the Canadiens originally drafted Plasse, he got his start in the NHL with the St.-Louis Blues, before jumping back to the Canadiens, then the Kansas City Scouts, the Pittsburgh Penguins, the Colorado Rockies and ending his career in 1982 with the Québec Nordiques.

First and Only Goaltender to Win Back-to-Back Hart Trophies

With GAAs of 2.27 in 1997 and 2.09 in 1998, it is not hard to see why Dominik Hasek was voted as the most valuable player (MVP) in the NHL two years in a row. During those two years, Hasek helped the Buffalo Sabres become one of the premiere clubs in the National Hockey League.

First Goaltender to Lose a Game without Letting In a Goal

It wasn't his fault, but Mario Gosselin will forever be attached to an unfortunate statistical anomaly.

Near the end of a Los Angeles Kings-Edmonton Oilers duel, the Kings netminder Kelly Hrudey was injured late in the third period and backup goaltender Mario Gosselin was called upon to finish out the remaining minutes of the game. The Kings were down 6-5 with time ticking by slowly, and they were forced to pull Gosselin to try for the equalizing goal only to see the Oilers slide the puck into the empty net to take a 7-5 lead. After Gosselin resumed his position in goal, the Kings potted a goal to come within one but it wasn't enough, and the Oilers won the game by a final score of 7-6. Seeing as Gosselin was the goaltender in the books for the Oilers seventh goal, he was charged with the loss even though he never allowed a single puck in the net.

First Russian Goaltender in the Hall of Fame

The world first got a good look at Vladislav Tretiak at the 1972 Summit Series. Scouting reports all indicated that the Soviet goaltender was the weakest part of the team and suffered from inconsistent play and a weak glove hand. However, the scout who filed that report had only seen Tretiak play one game in which he let in nine goals. The 20-year-old Tretiak had seen action with the Soviets in the world championships and in the Olympics and had performed better than the scouting reports suggested. Despite his confidence in Tretiak's ability to stop the Canadians in the Summit Series, one veteran goaltender thought the young Soviet could use a few tips on how to play against Canada's potent offence. Before the opening game in Montréal, Tretiak received a visitor in the Soviet dressing room. It was none other than goaltending legend Jacques Plante, and the first thing that he said to the young player was, "Steady strain. That is the fate of us goaltenders."

Plante, who was known for keeping actual books on the habits of the league's best shooters, gave Tretiak a detailed account on how to play each of Canada's best scorers. The tutorial seemed to help as the Soviets went on to defeat Canada 7-3 in the opening game. After the game, Canada's Peter Mahovlich said that Tretiak had played so well and knew all his moves like he had known him since he was a kid. To this day, Tretiak cannot figure out why Plante decided to help him.

"I'm still puzzled by what motivated him to do that," said Tretiak. "He probably felt sorry for me, the little guy, in whom Esposito was going to shoot holes."

The majority of the talk in the Canadian dressing room after the game was how they were going to solve the Tretiak dilemma. They knew the

20-year-old was still developing, but he was still proving to be a problem for Canada's top scorers. Tretiak was the obvious difference in the series and frustrated Canada's best for the entire eight games before Paul Henderson ended Tretiak's hopes with his famous game, and series-winning, goal.

Up until Henderson's famous goal, Tretiak and his constant ability to frustrate Team Canada was the talk of the entire tournament. After the Summit Series, the Soviet player the accolades kept coming his way with more brilliant performances.

"If there is a comparison to an NHL goalie I would make for Tretiak, it would be Terry Sawchuk," said Paul Henderson.

Tretiak was not as adventurous as Sawchuk, but he had incredible lightning quick reflexes and amazing agility. On more than one occasion, when a Canadian player thought he had Tretiak beat, suddenly a pad or glove would flash across the goal mouth to make the save. He had incredible patience when facing a shooter and always let them make the first move. He never guessed at what the player might do because, if he was wrong, the shooter would have an open net. With each level he attained, Tretiak stepped up to every challenge and seemed to get better and better as time went on.

In his time playing with the Soviet national team, Tretiak won three Olympic gold medals, one silver medal, ten world championships and countless other tournaments. There was just one thing left in his career that he had yet to accomplish—a spot on an NHL team.

By 1983, National Hockey League managers were well acquainted with Tretiak's work, but no team was more interested than the Montréal Canadiens, who saw fit to draft him 143rd overall that year. After leading the Soviet team to another gold medal at the 1984 Olympic Games in Sarajevo, Tretiak was sure that the USSR would release him to play in the National Hockey League, but travel restrictions kept him from ever testing himself in the North American market. Deeply angered by his country's refusal to allow him to play, Tretiak announced his retirement from hockey at the age of 32.

Tretiak said, "I was ready to come here for so long, and I think I would have done well. I've dedicated my whole life to hockey, and I would have given playing in the NHL 150%."

Despite never playing a single game for a North American professional team, Tretiak became the first European to be inducted into the Hockey Hall of Fame in 1989 for his contributions to the game of hockey. Tretiak finally did make it into the NHL, as a goaltender coach rather than as a player, when the Chicago Black Hawks hired him in 1990 to mentor a rookie goalie by the name of Eddie Belfour. Tretiak still runs a hockey school for goaltenders, passing down his wealth of experience gained over his illustrious career to a new generation.

First Goaltender to Nearly Die on National Television

Buffalo Sabres goaltender Clint Malarchuk came close to losing his life on March 22, 1989 when St. Louis Blues forward Steve Tuttle collided with a Sabres defenceman and was sent flying through the air at Malarchuk. In the collision Tuttle's skate sliced into Malarchuk's neck severing his jugular vein. Were it not for the quick thinking of trainer Jim Pizzutelli, who slowed the loss of blood until doctors could operate, Malarchuk would have died that night.

Chapter Three

Forwards

First Superstar of Hockey

Frank McGee was the first superstar in the game of hockey. The nephew of the famous Canadian politician D'Arcy McGee, Frank was a natural born athlete excelling in all sports, but hockey was his passion. Not long after taking up the sport, McGee quickly made a name for himself as the star of hockey's elite team, the Ottawa Silver Seven. McGee's most famous moment came in 1905, when his star-studded Ottawa club met a ragtag team from Dawson City, Yukon, in a battle for the right to be named the champions of Lord Stanley's Cup. In the first game of the series McGee scored only one goal although his team won the game 9-2. After that first game, all anyone could talk about was how the Dawson goaltender frustrated the great Frank McGee time and time again. This did not sit well with McGee. More determined than ever McGee returned in game two with one purpose in mind. He scored four goals in the first half (games at the time were played in two 30 minute halves), and in the second half he exploded, scoring eight goals in under eight minutes, adding two in the dying minutes of the game for an incredible total of 14 goals in one game. No player has come close to beating or tying McGee's record and no player ever will.

The First 50 Goals

Although the record has already been broken several times since Maurice Richard established the 50 goals in 50 games plateau, it is that first time a record once thought impossible to reach is beaten that people remember and that the history books always talk about.

Former Montréal Canadiens scoring ace "Phantom" Joe Malone, who potted an amazing 44 goals in 20 games in 1918, held the previous single season scoring record. As amazing as Malone's feat was, hockey was different in the first few years of the NHL. Rules favoured more open style games where offensive talents like Malone flourished. Scoring 50 goals in 50 games became the new measure for the scoring aces to break and none did it with more style than a young 23-year-old Montréal Canadiens forward named Maurice Richard.

By mid-season 1944-45, teamed with Elmer Lach and Toe Blake (aptly nicknamed the "punch" line), Richard had managed 29 goals in 27 games. Attention suddenly turned to the fiery young forward as people began to believe that the record could be broken if he could only stay on pace. Richard knew it was up to him to make good on the reputation he was building as a goal-scoring forward who would not be pushed around. He had many doubters early on in his career, and this was his year to shine.

The doubters were quickly silenced. After all, Richard was the one who actually carried players on his back and scored goals. "Over the years, people have asked me whether it was true that I actually scored a goal while carrying an opponent on my back, and the answer is 'yes'," remarked Richard.

The amazing goal happened when the Canadiens were playing the Detroit Red Wings and, as Maurice Richard broke free into the neutral zone he had only to get around the large Red Wing defence-man Earl Siebert to have a clear path to the net. As Siebert cut across the ice to try and stop Richard from having a clear path to the net, he realized that he could not get in front of the speedy Montréal forward so he did the next best thing. As Richard crossed into the Red Wings defensive zone,

Siebert wrapped his arms around the Rocket's shoulder trying to slow him down so that he could poke the puck off his stick. The crowd at the Forum gasped as Siebert jumped on Richard's back, trying anything to haul him down. Bearing the extra weight on his back, the sound of his skates breaking the ice with each step could be heard in the stunned silence of the Forum. Nothing was going to stop the Rocket.

"I felt as if I might cave in. The goaltender moved straight out for me, and somehow I managed to jab the puck between his legs while Siebert kept riding my back!" exclaimed Richard after the game.

In the Detroit locker room, Coach Jack Adams laid into his defenceman for not stopping Richard on the play, to which Siebert replied, "Listen Mr. Adams, I weigh over 200 pounds. Any guy who can carry me on his back from the blue line to the net deserves to score a goal."

After that game, Richard was an instant fan favourite. Break the 50-goal plateau, and he would become a legend.

By March 18, 1945, the final game of the season, Richard had reached 49 goals and everybody was watching to see if the Rocket could reach 50. The Canadiens were playing the Boston Bruins that night at the Boston Garden arena in front of an expectant crowd. Richard knew this was his last chance to score the goal, and if he didn't it would be a statistic that would haunt him for the rest of his career as a side note in hockey history. However, by the end of the second period it looked as if Richard would not get his record-setting goal. The Bruins were playing a tight game and began pressing hard near the end of the third period with the score 3-2 in favour of the Habs. Richard's teammates knew that his chances to score were dwindling, and they were going to everything possible to help him get his 50th goal. With just over two minutes left Richard finally got his chance.

Rushing across the blue line for one last chance, Richard and Elmer Lach set their sights on Boston goaltender Harvey Bennett. Trying to draw the goaltender and defenceman away from Richard, Lach cut in front of the net and tried to feather a pass to the Rocket, but the Bruins defenceman crashed into Lach, sending him underneath a mess of arms and legs near the goaltender's crease. Somehow the puck managed to find its way onto Richard's stick, and he simply poked it into the empty net for his 50th goal. Bennett immediately ran to the referee to protest that Lach had purposely interfered with him in the crease but had no luck convincing him of the obstruction, and the goal stood. The Canadiens bench cleared, and they swarmed around their star player. Québec's new icon had done it again.

Author Roch Carrier put the feeling of the province best when he wrote, "When Richard scored his 50 goals, he gave us all hope. French Canadiens are no longer to be condemned to be hewers of wood and drawers of water, to be servants, employees. We, too, are champions of the world."

Although Richard never again reached the 50-goal plateau, his record still stands out as one of the most amazing moments in hockey history. It wasn't until 1981 that the feat was equalled by the New York Islanders Mike Bossy and then smashed by Wayne Gretzky, who scored 50 goals in 39 games.

First Riot over a Player

By the time the 1954-55 NHL season started, Maurice Richard's temper was well known to league management, referees and players on other teams who often tried to exploit his push-button rage. None were more aware of the Rocket's misdeeds than league president Clarence Campbell. The two men, Campbell and the Rocket, had butted heads on a number of issues. The mistrust and dislike between them became the catalyst for the Richard riots of March 1955.

In December, Richard was forced to apologize to President Campbell for a series of articles that he had ghost written. The articles, published in a French-language paper, harshly criticized Campbell both personally and professionally. In the articles, Richard called Campbell the league's "Dictator" and charged him with openly cheering other teams when they scored against the predominantly French-Canadian Montréal Canadiens. Richard even goaded Campbell into taking action against him, saying, "If Mr. Campbell wants to throw me out of the league for daring to criticize him, let him do it." The incident cost Richard $1000 and a public apology but earned him a place in the heart of French-Canadian fans. They saw Richard as an "everyman" figure fighting against the elitist English establishment. It didn't hurt that he could score a goal like no one else.

Penalties were not enough to deter the Rocket as he continued to rack up fines for getting under Clarence Campbell's skin.

Another episode of the drama took place during a game against long-time rivals and Campbell favourites, the Toronto Maple Leafs. The clock was winding down on an exciting but relatively non-violent game between the Leafs and Canadiens. With just a few minutes remaining all hell broke loose when Richard became involved in a scuffle with Leafs forward Bob Bailey. Instead of swinging, Bailey tried to gouge out Richard's eyes. Richard lost his temper and went berserk with rage. He knocked two teeth out of Bailey's mouth.

Referee Red Storey remembered the incident in Dick Irvin's book *The Habs*, "Every time we'd get the Rocket straightened out he'd go over to the bench and Dick (Irvin Sr.) would give him another stick. When we saw the replay, he'd had five different sticks before it was over. He wasn't hunting for trouble any night. But I'll tell you, when trouble started, he finished it."

Richard was fined $250 for the incident. No matter how many fines he threw at Richard, Campbell knew it would not stop him from participating in another incident.

"For every $250 I fined him, Québec businessmen would send him $1000," said Campbell of Richard's popularity in Québec. "Richard could do no wrong in Québec. I was always the villain." He was right.

The events that led to the riots continued during a game between the Canadiens and the Boston Bruins on March 13, 1955. With only four games remaining in the regular season, the Canadiens wanted to end their rivalry with the Bruins on a high note, but Boston had a 4-2 lead late in the third period. At this point in the game, Boston defenceman Hal Laycoe and Richard met on the ice for one of the most infamous fights in hockey.

"On this particular night, the Bruins were really up for us. They laid on the lumber at every opportunity, and by the time the game had reached the end of the first period, we were a very bruised bunch of men," noted Richard, as he looked back on the Laycoe incident.

The incident happened when Laycoe and Richard both rushed into a corner after the puck and collided in a mess of arms and sticks. Richard got the worst of the hit. As he was falling to the ice, his stick caught Laycoe on the head, opening up a gash that poured blood. Laycoe, furious at the assault, swung his stick at Richard several times, catching him on the side of the head and opening a "bleeder" that trickled down his face into his eyes. When Richard saw the blood, he lost his cool. His eyes changed—he became a man on a mission and Laycoe was the target. The sticks started swinging. Some were aimed at shoulders, some at heads—others were even two-handed. Hoping to stop the fight before anyone was seriously hurt, linesman Cliff Thompson jumped in and tried to break up the fight.

When Thompson grabbed Richard in an attempt to hold him back from Laycoe, Richard broke free and lunged at the Bruin defenceman several times. Fed up with having the linesman hold him back Richard warned the linesman not to grab him from behind again. Thompson, however, did so and pinned Richard down on the ice. This sent Richard into a fury. Seeing his teammate pinned by the linesman, Canadiens defenceman Doug Harvey knocked Thompson off the enraged Richard. Richard jumped up and punched the linesman twice in the face. Richard felt the punch was deserved—after all, he had warned Thompson.

"He wouldn't listen. That's why I hit him," said Richard.

What is often omitted from the story is that Thompson, at one time, had been a defenceman for the Boston Bruins. Whether this was a factor in the melee is not known, but it is interesting to note that Thompson did not officiate another game in the National Hockey League. For his actions, Richard was thrown out of the game. He knew he would be having another meeting with Campbell about this incident.

On the train ride back to Montréal, the team was ominously silent. Richard sat quietly staring out the window feeling that his actions were justified, but he expected the league's reaction wouldn't help his team. Team owners across the league condemned Richard as a loose cannon who should be dealt with harshly. It was left to NHL president Clarence Campbell to decide how Richard should be punished.

French media in Montréal were in an uproar over having the fate of their hero in the hands of Campbell, who was known for his personal dislike of Richard, the Canadiens and French Canadians in general. It was a feeling that had been building in the city for some time. The French majority were protesting social and wage discrepancies between them and their English counterparts. The city had seen a number of demonstrations by the French majority, and the Richard affair seemed ready to light the fuse on the tense situation.

After some deliberation, Campbell came down with the verdict in an official 18-paragraph document that spelled out the reasons for his next course of action. All the Montréal fans needed to read was the final sentence: "In the result, Richard will be suspended from all games, both league and playoff, for the balance of the current season."

Front-page headlines in the French Montréal papers echoed the sentiment prevalent in the city:

La Presse: *"Too Harsh a Penalty: Mayor Drapeau hoping for a review of sentence."*

Montréal-Matin: *"Victim of yet another injustice, the worst ever, Maurice Richard will play no more this season."*

At Richard's home, phone calls of support came in from people he knew and many he didn't.

"Rocket! We're going to get even with Campbell. There's going to be a lot of trouble at the Forum tonight."

"It's an injustice! Campbell will get what is coming to him!"

Campbell was getting phone calls at his home but of a less supportive nature. Despite the death threats, Campbell was not deterred from enforcing his decision on Richard's suspension. He even announced he would appear at the next Canadiens' game at the Forum.

"It is my right and my duty to be present at the game both as a citizen and as president of the league," said Campbell defiantly.

On the evening of March 17, 1955, the Canadiens were taking on their long-time rivals, the Detroit Red Wings, who were two points behind them in the overall standings. Among the 16,000 fans at the Forum was a nervous but defiant Clarence Campbell. Outside, angry fans began to gather in ever-increasing numbers, chanting slogans supporting Richard and denouncing Campbell:

"Vive Richard!" "Campbell Drop Dead!" "Richard, the Persecuted!"

With the game underway Campbell took his seat to a chorus of boos and had to dodge occasional tomatoes thrown at him. As the game went on, the crowd focused less on what was happening on the ice and more on the league president sitting smugly in the stands. A young man wearing a leather jacket approached Campbell near the end of the first period under the pretence of shaking the president's hand but instead punched him several times before police intervened. Then a tear gas bomb exploded sending a cloud of acrid smoke through the Forum that sent patrons rushing for the exits.

The 250 police officers were not able to control the chaos as thousands of irate fans exited the building and joined the thousands of angry protesters outside the Forum. The excitement carried outside sparked the angry crowd that quickly turned into a mob. The mob moved down Ste-Catherine Street, smashing windows, setting fires and overturning cars. When the violence died down at 3:00 AM, the west end of downtown Montréal had been laid to waste.

Richard was appalled by the violence of that night. Yet, he felt the affair would not have reached the peak it did had Campbell not made an appearance at the Forum.

"What Campbell did was no more sensible than waving a red flag in front of an angry bull," said Richard.

Urged on by Frank Selke, the general manager of the Montréal Canadiens, Richard spoke on the local radio in both languages the morning after the riot and appealed for calm. "I will take my punishment," he said, "and come back next year."

That morning, the citizens of Montréal were ashamed of what they had done to their city in the name of their hero who did not condone such actions. Adding further insult, the Detroit Red Wings beat the Canadiens in the Stanley Cup finals that year.

With Maurice back the next year, the Canadiens finished on top of the league and won the first of what would be five straight Stanley Cups. L'Affair Richard, as it is called in French, secured Maurice Richard's status as a cultural icon in Québec and a legend in hockey that has yet to see his equal.

First "Hat Trick"
The tradition of throwing hats onto the ice after a player scores three goals hasn't always been part of the game. Before 1946 scoring three

goals was just that, three goals, and not a hat trick, as it is more commonly known as today. The term came about in 1946 when fashionable Chicago Black Hawks forward Alex Kaleta walked into a local haberdashery in Toronto owned by Sammy Taft. Kaleta bet the hatter that if he scored three goals in the game that night against the Maple Leafs, Taft would have to give him a hat of his choice for free. Knowing that scoring three goals was quite unlikely, Taft took the young Black Hawks forward's bet. Kaleta scored his three goals that night and walked into Taft's hat store the next day to collect his winnings. When the newspapers got wind of the story and quoted Taft saying, "Yeah, that was some trick he pulled to get that hat," scoring three goals in one game became known from that day on as a "hat trick." Ever the smart businessman, Taft used the publicity from the Kaleta story to promote his business, and every time a Toronto player scored three goals he would give them a free hat. The term has stuck ever since, and now the crowd supplies the hats for the players by throwing them on the ice after a hat trick.

First 20-Goal Scorer

For those who know their hockey history, Joe Malone was one of the best hockey players of his time and one of the purest goal scorers in hockey history. For those who might have never heard of the "Phantom" Joe Malone, please take the time to learn his story.

Born Maurice Joseph Malone in Québec City, on February 28, 1890, Joe Malone took to the game from an early age. However, there were some early issues.

When he was just taking his first few steps onto the ice, he was not big enough yet to play with older boys, but once he grew a few more inches, Malone quickly developed into a skilled player. In those games he played as a boy where there were no real rules or strategy, it was everybody against one player, and it was there that Malone quickly learned his lessons. And as there was often a lack of nets or a willing goaltender, the purpose of those large games was basically whoever could hold onto the puck longest. Blessed with natural speed, it was Malone that often left a panting trail of children behind him.

Years later with the Montréal Canadiens, fans noticed that this English bloke guarded the puck like a piece of meat from a hungry pack of wolves. Malone was said to skate like a ghost because he could skate through any defensive roadblock at top speeds and score before the defenders or goaltender knew what had happened. Fans immediately took to him, and his fame grew once the press had dubbed him "The Phantom."

When he joined the Montréal Canadiens, his reputation had already been forged during his days in the National Hockey Association as the Québec Bulldogs' star player. His scoring in games was so prolific that he was allowed to score nine goals in a Stanley Cup game that had his Québec Bulldogs defending their championship against a hopelessly outclassed Sydney Miners.

Malone eventually joined the Montréal Canadiens after the National Hockey Association folded in 1917. It was the perfect team for the type of player that liked to take control of the puck and play open hockey. Teamed up with other legendary hockey player Newsy Lalonde, Malone was the Canadiens primary weapon in that inaugural NHL season. He was so good that by January 12, 1918, not even 30 days into the NHL schedule, Malone scored his 20th goal of the season becoming the first NHL player to do so. The game was against the Ottawa Senators, and when the first puck dropped, Malone had only 15 goals on the season, but by the end whistle he'd put five past Ottawa goalie Clint Benedict and carried the team to a 9-4 victory. When the season ended, Malone had tallied 44 goals in just 20 games. That's an average of 2.2 goals per game; not even

Wayne Gretzky scored at that rate during his prime in the early 1980s.

Double Hat Trick + One

Well the story of Joe Malone does not end after his first year of NHL action. After leaving hockey for a year, Malone came back with the Québec Bulldogs for the start of the 1919-20 NHL season. The Bulldogs were simply an awful team, and Malone was their sole bright spot. They won just four games out of 24 that year and only managed to score 91 goals. Malone for his part scored 39 of those goals.

His best game of that season came against the Toronto St-Patricks on January 31, 1920. Before a sparse crowd of only 1200 people, the animosity between the St-Pats and the Bulldogs was evident from the drop of the puck, and Malone gained control early. His first goal of the game came on a brilliant rush down the left wing, zipping through the Toronto defence and snapping a shot into the right-hand corner of the net. Later in the period, with his teammates buzzing around the mouth of the goal, Malone let go a shot from the blue line that tickled the twine but was immediately called off by the referee. In the mess of legs and sticks, apparently one of the players had kicked the puck in. Malone knew the referee had made the wrong call and vowed to double his efforts in the second and third periods.

Using the disallowed goal as motivation, Malone scored two more goals in the second for a hat trick. But it wasn't until late in the third period that Malone began to pick up the pace. Dancing around the defence and embarrassing the Toronto goaltender, Malone added four more goals for a total of seven in a 10-6 thrashing of the St-Pats. No player has since equalled or broken that mark.

Malone might have got credit for a few assists, but at the time, assists were not counted as seriously as they are in modern hockey.

First NHL Stanley Cup Finals Hat Trick

Alf "Dutch" Skinner was one of the top players during the frontier days of hockey, when the hockey was violent, the travel was exhausting and the pay was a pittance. Skinner simply played for the love of hockey, and he showed his devotion to the game by playing in the top leagues at the beginning of the 20th century starting at the age of 16.

After several years in the Ontario Hockey Association, he joined up with the Toronto Shamrocks of the National Hockey Association in

1914 and would eventually make the move to the NHL in 1917 to play for the Toronto Arenas.

Skinner was a solid player for the Arenas, but in his time with the team he was overshadowed by the flashy standouts Reg Noble and Corb Denneny. But Skinner stole back some of that spotlight during an important second game of the first Stanley Cup finals versus the Vancouver Millionaires when he scored the first hat trick in the finals. Toronto later finished off the Millionaires in five games to become the first NHL team to win the Stanley Cup.

First Player to Score 3 Goals in 21 Seconds

In the early 1950s, an era dominated by the Detroit Red Wings and the Montréal Canadiens, the lowly Chicago Black Hawks floated near the bottom of the league and had few great moments to cheer about. But hockey is a strange sport, and every now and then even the worst team in the league might get its moment in the sun. For the Black Hawks, more precisely Hawk forward Bill Mosienko, that moment came in during the 1951-52 season.

Nothing had gone right for the Black Hawks for over a decade, and that season continued the disappointing trend of yet another losing season.

With just a few games remaining in the regular season, the Hawks were yet again going to miss out on the playoffs and were simply playing out the season trying to hold their heads up high.

The Black Hawks were clearly not going to make the playoffs, and the glory years of Bobby Hull and Stan Mikita were still several years away. The only shining light for the Hawks was a large right-winger with a passion for the game named Bill Mosienko.

Since his 1941 NHL debut, Mosienko had been a solid position player who could score goals and play a defensive game when called upon. Management had placed a lot of faith in the young forward that he would develop into a player of Maurice Richard or Ted Lindsay's character, but with such a weak team as the Hawks, Mosienko's fortunes were going the way of his team's.

Despite the odds stacked against him, Mosienko's most memorable year came at the 1952 season end. He was set to finish seventh in the league in scoring, and in the final game of the season (March 23, 1952), Mosienko secured a place for himself in the annals of hockey history.

The game was not a highly anticipated affair since the Black Hawks and the New York Rangers were both going to miss the playoffs and were simply playing the game for pride. The game got underway, and it was apparent from the beginning that the New York Rangers had complete control of the game. By the end of the third period, the Rangers had amassed a 6-2 lead. At the start of the third period, the Rangers fans at the Madison Square Garden that night sat back in their seats comfortable with the four-goal lead with just 20 minutes to go. However, at the six-minute mark things turned in the Black Hawks' favour when Bill Mosienko took control. The first goal came at the 6:09 mark in the third when Black-hawk centre Gus Bodnar won the face-off and got the puck to Mosienko, who managed to sneak in behind the defence. He beat Rangers goaltender Lorne Anderson on the low side with a quick wrist shot. A few seconds later on an identical play, Mosienko scored his second goal. Rangers fans began to move nervously in their seats as the momentum began to shift. Mosienko's third goal came at the 6:30 minute mark after Bodnar won the face-off and got the puck to his defenceman, who noticed that once again Mosienko had gotten behind the defence and fed him a tape to tape pass. Lorne Anderson could not do anything as Mosienko deked around him and buried the puck in the upper part of the net. Mosienko had scored three goals in 21 seconds, a mark that still stands to this day. The only player to come close was Jean Béliveau of the 1955 Montréal Canadiens who scored three power play goals in 44 seconds. Mosienko's line mate Gus Bodnar also went into the record books for the fastest three assists. Incidentally, the Black Hawks went on to win the game 7-6 on a pair of goals late in the period scored by Syd Finney.

First Player to Score over 70 Goals in One Season

At one time in the NHL, scoring over 50 goals in a season was considered a heroic feat but 60 goals or even 70 was considered almost impossible. It took several decades, but the impossible was finally achieved when Boston Bruins forward Phil Esposito scored an incredible 76 goals in one season. Paired up with players like Ken Hodge, Bobby Orr and John Bucyk it is understandable how he achieved such a total.

First Player to Score over 90 Goals in One Season

In 1981-82 a young Wayne Gretzky scored an incredible 92 goals completely smashing Phil Esposito's single season mark of 76 goals in the 1970-71 season with the Bruins. That year, Gretzky also became the first person to break the 200-point mark in NHL history.

First Player to Record 10 Points in One Game

During his first two years with the Toronto Maple Leafs, Darryl Sittler did not get the debut he would have liked, scoring only 25 goals. With the new 1973-74 season, Sittler turned things around and became on of the top players in the NHL at the time.

A few years later (in 1976) Sittler would have his best year in the NHL. The first highlight for the Leafs forward came on February 7, 1976, when the Toronto Maple Leafs took on the Boston Bruins. There was no special attention brought to the game before the puck dropped; it was just a regular season match-up between two teams who were fighting for a favourable position in the coming playoffs. Boston had the upper hand on the Leafs that season, but this game would prove to be different.

From the moment the puck was dropped, it was clear that the Leafs had control. Boston could not get a play started, and the Leafs pounded the Bruins net with shot after shot. Sittler scored six goals and assisted on four leading the game—a record that has survived even the Gretzky and Lemieux years.

Recalling the game, Sittler said: "As much as the fans fault [Boston goaltender Dave] Reece for what happened, it was simply a night where every shot and pass I made seemed to pay off in a goal. I hit the corners a couple of times, banking shots in off the post. The kid was screened on a couple of goals and had no chance. He didn't really flub one goal. On the tenth point, I banked a shot in from behind the net off Brad Park's leg."

The Leafs handed the Bruins one of their most embarrassing losses of the season and also shattered the confidence of the rookie goaltender, who was unfortunately dubbed "in-the-wrong-place-at-the-wrong-time-Reece." Reece would never play another game in the NHL.

In the playoffs that year, Sittler had another game that went down in the record books. In the first round of the playoffs, the Leafs faced the tough Philadelphia Flyers and the excellent goaltending of Bernie Parent. The hard checking of the Flyers and the solid goaltending of Parent did not stop Sittler from having another record game. He scored five goals to tie an NHL record. Unfortunately, the Leafs did not make it any further in the playoffs. But Sittler's banner year was not over.

He later secured his place in the history books during the first Canada Cup when Canada found itself in overtime against Czechoslovakia. They could not break the 4-4 tie in the back-and-forth game, making overtime necessary to decide the winner of the first-ever Canada Cup. With national pride on the line, Canada battled to get the puck past the Czechoslovakian net-minder but could not break the deadlock until the 11th minute of the first overtime period. Sittler proved to be the hero again when he picked up the puck at centre ice and streaked down on the left side. The Montréal Forum crowd could sense something coming as Sittler broke through the defence, and with a slight deke, put the puck past the outstretched Czechoslovakian goalie for the winning goal.

Although Sittler never won a Stanley Cup, he continued to lead the Leafs to several successful seasons. They came close in the 1978 playoffs, only to be eliminated in the semi-finals. In 16 seasons in the NHL, Sittler finished his career with 1121 total points and was inducted into the Hockey Hall of Fame in 1989.

First Black Player in the NHL

He had been waiting all his life for the moment he first put on the Boston Bruins jersey and could call himself a professional hockey player. He had first put on a pair of skates at the age of three and had been dreaming of this moment all his life. But the road to the NHL was not an easy one for any black hockey player during the late '50s and early '60s.

In today's multi-ethnic, multi-national hockey league, it seems ridiculous that a player would be excluded on the sole condition of the colour of his skin, but that was the pervasive attitude in the days before Willie O'Ree broke into the NHL. There were plenty of black players in the minor hockey leagues around North America, but none had ever broken into the NHL. A young Toronto native named Herb Carnegie, a player with the Québec Aces of the Québec Senior Hockey League during the 1940s, was recognized as one of the best players on his team but was denied even a chance a trying out for an NHL club simply because of the colour of his skin. Toronto owner Conn Smythe even told the young player once, "Herb, I'd sign you in a minute if I could turn you white." The talent was there just not the will for management to break the colour barrier.

O'Ree finally got his chance when the Boston Bruins called him up from the minors for only two games played against the Montréal Canadiens starting on January 18, 1958. He never scored during his brief stay with the Bruins that year, but he had achieved something that changed the game forever. Like Jackie Robinson had done 10 years earlier, the colour barrier had been broken, but it still wasn't easy to be black in the National Hockey League. "I know Robinson had it much tougher," said O'Ree.

O'Ree was called back up to the Bruins two years later for the final half of the 1960-61 season. This time O'Ree was with the team as they travelled to other cities, and that's when he began to hear racial slurs thrown at him almost every night. But in the Bruins locker room, it was a different story.

"They were mean to me in places like Detroit and New York, too. But never in Boston," said O'Ree in Brian McFarlane's book *Best of the Original Six.* "I'll never forget how my teammates there—men like Johnny Bucyk, Doug Mohns, Charlie Burns and Don McKenney—took care of me. They accepted me totally. All of them had class."

When asked about the new addition to the team, Bruins coach Milt Schmidt said, "He isn't black, he's a Bruin."

There were always players on the other teams that weren't as welcoming to a black player in the NHL. O'Ree was constantly being taunted about his colour by other players and even fans who would curse at him every time he touched the puck. One night in Chicago, the taunting got out of hand after an incident involving O'Ree and Blackhawk forward Eric Nesterenko.

Trouble started when Nesterenko went into the corner to check O'Ree off the puck and gave him the butt-end of his stick right into his mouth knocking out two teeth in the process. When O'Ree retaliated by nailing him on the head with his stick, the crowd began hurling racial slurs at the bleeding Boston defenceman. The referee had no choice but to throw both players out of the game, but O'Ree was having trouble getting off the ice because the fans were throwing anything they could get their hands on at the Boston forward. A police escort had to be called in to usher O'Ree off the ice and out of the arena before the game ended to prevent any further violence.

"Those Chicago fans were livid. They were ready to murder me," said O'Ree.

O'Ree's National Hockey League career only lasted 45 games before he was traded to the Montréal Canadiens where he never got the chance to prove what he could do. He spent the rest of his career in the minor leagues where he excelled twice winning the Western Hockey League scoring title.

Although he only played 45 games, O'Ree opened up the game for a whole new generation of kids who might never have got the chance to play in the NHL if he hadn't crossed the line first.

Timeline of Black Hockey History

1830s-40s: African Canadians began to participate in the early form of hockey in Nova Scotia.

1880s: Black communities in eastern Canada began to form separate sports clubs as they were banned from participating in the established "white" leagues.

1890s: Coloured hockey teams began to organize in eastern Canada.

1899: Hipple "Hippie" Galloway became the star player for the Woodstock hockey team of the Central Hockey Association. But after a racially motivated incident, Galloway left Canada to join an all-black team in the United States prompting one local Woodstock writer to comment, "An effort should be made to keep Hippie in town. Our hockey team needs him."

March 9, 1899: On this date the (all-black) Halifax Eurekas took on the (all-white) Halifax Chebuctos in the first recorded racially divided hockey game. The Eurekas won the game by a final score of 9-7.

1900: The Coloured Hockey League of the Maritimes was formed. The league was founded by Henry Sylvester Williams, James Robinson and James A.R. Kinney to promote and give a public face to the black community in the Maritimes.

Team names often referenced the past slave trade and the Underground Railroad that brought people up from the Southern United States to the Maritimes. The Dartmouth Jubilees was a reference to the "Jubilee of Emancipation," the date when slavery was abolished throughout the British Empire. The Hammonds Plains Moss Backs name was inspired by the code used in the Underground Railroad that informed freed slaves that they were headed in the right direction because moss grows on the north side of trees.

1938: Toronto Maple Leaf owner Conn Smythe told young African Canadian junior hockey phenom Herb Carnegie, "I'd take you tomorrow if you could turn white."

1948: The New York Rangers invited Herb Carnegie to their training camp for a try out and offer him a spot in their minor league system. He refused the offer that would have seen his salary cut in half from what he was making as a semi-professional.

1950-53: Herb Carnegie played with the Québec Aces of the Québec Senior Hockey League alongside future legends such as Jean Béliveau, Marcel Bonin and Jean-Guy Talbot.

January 17, 1958: Willie O'Ree became the first African Canadian to play in the NHL when he was called up by the Boston Bruins from the minors to fill in for an injured player.

January 1, 1961: In a game against the Montréal Canadiens, late in the third period with the score tied, Willie O'Ree broke across the Canadiens line and let go a low hard shot that beat the goaltender and won the Bruins the game. It was the first goal by a black player in the NHL and O'Ree's first goal in the NHL.

1974: Mike Marson became only the second back player in NHL history when he suited up for the Washington Capitals. Later that season, when Marson and teammate Bill Riley dressed for a game on December 26, it became the first time in the NHL that more than one black player appeared in a game.

1978: Tony McKegney joined the NHL with the Buffalo Sabres. He became the first black star player, scoring over 20 goals per season through most of his career. With the St. Louis Blues in 1987-88 season, he scored 40 goals.

1981: Grant Fuhr became the first starting goaltender of African decent in the NHL.

1984: Grant Fuhr became the first black player to have his name engraved on the Stanley Cup when his Edmonton Oilers beat the New York Islanders to take the championship.

1989: Dirk Graham became the first player with African ancestry to captain an NHL team. From 1989 to 1995, Graham was captain of the Chicago Black Hawks.

1995: Jerome Iginla became the highest draft player of African decent when he was selected 11th overall by the Dallas Stars.

2002: Iginla recorded the best statistical season ever by a player of African descent scoring 52 goals and 44 assists for 96 points. That same year Iginla became the first black man to win a Winter Olympic medal when he helped the Canadian National Hockey Team to a gold over the United States.

2003: Grant Fuhr became the first black player inducted into the Hall of Fame

The First Native Player in the NHL

While he holds the distinction of being the first Native hockey player to break the National Hockey League colour barrier, Fred Sasakamoose did not have a long and privileged career. Yet, what makes his story compelling are the struggles he had to endure along the way simply to get his foot in the door and get the chance he wanted. He got that chance and left behind a legacy for all the young Native kids who grew up and wanted to be hockey players. In Fred Sasakamoose they saw a possibility where before there wasn't one.

The official NHL record book states that Fred
Sasakamoose played 11 games for the Chicago
Black Hawks, had no goals, no assists, and accu-
mulated six minutes in penalties. Fred Sasakamoose was not unlike many young players
coming up through the minor leagues. He made
the frequent long bus trips across the Canadian
winter landscape to play, got the required stitches
and chipped teeth that were an integral part of
minor league hockey. Yet Fred Sasakamoose was
always different. It was on those trips through the
Canadian countryside that the exploits of a Native
hockey player began to spread. Possessed with
incredible speed and a fierce determination to get
to the front of the net, he was often called the
"Indian Rocket Richard." When he finally made
it to the big leagues, he had proven that a Native
player was just as good as any other. He might
have only played in 11 NHL games, but what the
numbers do not reveal is what Fred Sasakamoose's accomplishment meant to the history of
the NHL and to all Native peoples. He opened
the door for generations of young Native kids to
follow in his footsteps. Without his efforts slug-
ging through all of those small towns in the
minors and playing in those 11 games the long
line of great Native hockey players such as
George Armstrong, Bryan Trottier, Theoren

Fleury and Carey Price might never have been possible.

Growing up on the Big River Reserve in Saskatchewan in the 1930s and '40s, Fred Sasakamoose did not have much as a child growing up. While many children his same age began to discover hockey and their parents bought them a pair of skates and a hockey stick to play with, Sasakamoose grew up with little and had to resort to using tree branches for sticks and rocks for a puck.

Sasakamoose's upbringing was like many other Native kids during that time. Taken away from his parents at the age of five by the government, he was placed in a residential school. The aim was to give the Native children a chance at an education that they never would have received on a reserve, but what actually went on in those "schools" was far from a normal education.

While Sasakamoose did not have it as hard as some Native children, life in the residential school was not ideal. He was not allowed to speak his Native Cree language or to observe any cultural practices. Punishment for disobeying the rules was severe, and after morning classes, children were sent to work on the school's farm.

However, in among all the work there was still time to be a kid, and in the winter the only way to do that was to play hockey. The priests at the school were all from Montréal and, therefore, loved their hockey. Seven days a week, the priests coached those boys like they taught them in school, and all the extra discipline began to show in Sasakamoose's game as he quickly became the best hockey player in the school. The entire school benefited from the extra effort, and by the time he was 14 years old, Sasakamoose's team had won the Northern Saskatchewan Midget hockey championship in 1946, the first time a Native school had won the title.

Sasakamoose's skills on the ice got him noticed, and the Moose Jaw Canucks of the Western Hockey League soon came calling to sign him to their team for the start of the 1950-51 season. It wasn't easy going from the small town life of the reserve to a "white" city like Moose Jaw. There were racist comments all the time, but Sasakamoose just put his head down and tried to let his game speak for itself. By his second season in Moose Jaw, most of the hockey fans had quieted down with their inappropriate comments because Sasakamoose was by then one of the best players on the ice—so much so that the head coach nominated him as captain of the team. In his second year with the team, he had become the power centre of the team, scoring 19 goals and 22 assists in 42 games.

When he was 16 years old, the Chicago Black Hawks had already recognized the talent in Sasakamoose and had him sign a letter for $100, committing himself to the franchise when he came of age. At 20 years of age, Sasakamoose finally got that call.

"You have a dream. A dream to play in the NHL—couldn't go any higher. The Chicago Black Hawks got a hold of me. They said, 'You report to Toronto on Saturday night.' Being a Native in this world is very hard. I realized my dream: the NHL," said Sasakamoose, in an interview with Don Marks from his book *They Call me Chief.*

The transition from the small town Indian reserve to the skyscrapers of Toronto was a shock at first, but even more so was getting to meet legendary radio broadcaster Foster Hewitt. Sasakamoose had grown up listening to Hewitt's broadcast every Saturday night and could not believe he was getting the chance to talk to him. But the meeting was not how he had imagined. Speaking to Hewitt over the telephone, after dispensing with the usual greetings, Hewitt asked Sasakamoose how to pronounce his name. When Hewitt suggested "Saskatchewan-moose, Saskatoon-moose," in a condescending manner, Sasakamoose simply hung up the phone. It was a bold move for an NHL rookie to make, but Sasakamoose had his pride.

What was most notable about Fred Sasakamoose during his short stay in the NHL was that he was a hard worker, a deceptively fast skater and had one of the hardest slapshots in the NHL. But life in the big city proved to be too much for the kid from small town Saskatchewan. If the hustle of Moose Jaw had bothered him at first, imagine what the bright lights and fast pace of Chicago would do to a kid who grew up in a log cabin. He wanted to be near his family and his young wife. He played with the Black Hawks for the last 11 games of the 1953-54 season and returned home during the off-season.

Yet when it came time for him to return to training camp, Sasakamoose just didn't have what it took to survive away from his land and people, and he left the bright lights of the NHL for the Calgary Stampeders of the Western Hockey League. But even Calgary was too far from home for his liking, especially for his wife, so he hung up his skates.

But he never stayed completely away from the game; after all, to his people he was like Maurice Richard. He continued to play recreational games and established hockey schools to give Native youth a direction.

His time under the bright lights of the NHL may have been brief, but his impact on the game and for the history of his people was legendary.

First Slapshot

While Bobby Hull perfected the slapshot he was not the first to use this weapon with deadly skill. That honour belongs to the Montréal Canadiens Bernie "Boom Boom" Geoffrion (You might hazard to guess as to how he got his nickname.)

Born and raised in Montréal, Bernard Geoffrion naturally gravitated toward hockey as a youth, but the power forward whose name and number now hang in the rafters at the Bell Centre almost did not make it to the NHL. As a young and aspiring player, a coach told Bernie that he didn't have the skill that it would take to realize his dreams of making an NHL club. Luckily, Bernie possessed a fiery temperament that when challenged only prompted him to try harder.

"That made me mad," he remembered years later. "I was only a kid and then somebody tells me I can't make the NHL. I thought that maybe I'd show him something." And he did! Geoffrion played his junior career in Montréal and Laval and finally got his chance with the Montréal Canadiens in his first full season in 1952. His 30 goals and 24 assists were enough to earn him the Calder Trophy as rookie of the year. The Calder Trophy was certainly a memorable achievement but he had made a more lasting impression (especially among goaltenders) with his powerful slapshot.

When he broke into the league in 1952, the slapshot had not yet appeared in the NHL. Players were skilled wrist and snap shot artists, but the cannon slapshot had yet to appear. Along came Bernie, and goaltenders everywhere were praying for their lives. Pucks that used to come at them going a mere 50 to 60 mph were now speeding towards them closer to 80 and 90 mph.

It was a shot that he had been working since he was a kid playing on the outdoor rinks around Montréal. He noticed that when he put all his weight behind a shot that he had an easier time beating the goalies. Not only did it travel faster, but it also had the added effect of intimidating the opposition. Even when his shots missed the nets, the "boom" noise the puck made when it hit the boards reverberated around the rink, making goalies' knees shake. It wasn't much of a stretch for his friends to dub Geoffrion "Boom Boom"; one "Boom" for the sound of his stick hitting the puck and the other "Boom" for when he hit his target.

Geoffrion's shot was one of the ingredients that made the Canadiens so successful during his years with the team, and it helped him to become only the second person in NHL history (after Maurice Richard) to score 50 goals in one season when he hit the mark during the 1960-61 season. Bobby Hull eventually out slapped Geoffrion with his own devastating shot, but Geoffrion was the first to use it on such a grand and effective scale.

First Player to Score the Cycle

On December 30, 1988, Mario Lemieux scored five goals against the New Jersey Devils. Anyone who grew up watching Mario Lemieux play for the Pittsburgh Penguins knows very well that he could score goals in a multitude of ways, but on this particular night against the Devils the artist goal scorer showed off his true genius. As amazing as a five-goal game was, the fact that he scored each goal in a different way is incredible.

He did it by scoring a power play goal, shorthanded, even strength, empty net and penalty shot. No one has ever equalled or come close to scoring for the cycle. That's why he was the magnificent one.

First (and the last) Player to Win the Stanley Cup 11 Times

The Montréal Canadiens' Henri Richard played 20 seasons in the NHL. He was a solid offensive threat throughout most of those years and an integral part of the team's successes. Throughout his career, he always lived in the shadow of his older brother, Maurice, but the Rocket never accomplished one thing that Henri did. In 20 years in the NHL, Henri won the Stanley Cup an incredible 11 times. When he first joined the Canadiens in 1955, they won five straight. He added four more in the '60s and another two in the early '70s for a total of 11. Jean Béliveau comes in second for total Stanley Cup championships with 10. No player will ever equal that feat again.

The First to Play 964 Games in a Row

Most players are lucky to have a career that lasts 964 games, let alone to play them all in a row, but NHL iron man Doug Jarvis did just that through the 1970s and 1980s, on three different teams no less.

Chapter Four

Defencemen

First Defenceman to Lead NHL in Scoring

It doesn't happen often that a single player comes along and changes the way the game is played.

Many athletes in the position of the goaltender over the years have added to the development of the position, from Patrick Roy's butterfly style to Jacques Plante's use of the mask, but one goalie in particular was able to change the style of the game forever. There once was a time in the rules of hockey when goaltenders were penalized two minutes when they fell to the ice to make a save. All that changed with Clint Benedict, goaltender for the Ottawa Senators. The problem was that Benedict would always fall to the ice to make a save, and he was being penalized several times in a game. Frustrated at having to give out so many penalties to the acrobatic goaltender, the league finally changed the rules to allow goaltenders to fall to the ice and make a save any way they saw fit.

Wayne Gretzky forced teams to rethink their defensive systems after he led the Oilers through their golden years of the 1980s. During their reign through the '80s, the Edmonton Oilers scored the most goals by a team in one season with 446 in the 1983-84 season. The Oilers still hold the number two, three, four and five spots on the list, and all were scored during those fire-wagon years of the 1980s.

For the guys on defence, no player influenced the game more than the legendary Bobby Orr. Defence-men had always remained solid in their positions behind the forward line and rarely left the blue line to get a shot at the net. The defenceman was a reli-able position player who made passes and defended his zone against the other teams. If a defenceman managed to score 50 points in a season, he was considered a great asset to any team.

Bruins scouts got wind of a young defenceman who could defend his zone with the skill of Doug Harvey and could rush up the ice and score with the touch of Gordie Howe. During his days with the Oshawa Generals of the Ontario Hockey Association, Orr was one of the most effec-tive players on the ice. In his final year with the Generals, Orr recorded 38 goals and 56 assists in

47 games. His skills in the 1966 Memorial Cup final earned him an immediate spot on the Bruins roster when he made his professional debut later that year at the start of the 1966-67 NHL season.

Orr's impression on the league was immediate. He won the Calder Trophy for the league's best rookie and was named to his first of many All-Star games. He played excellent hockey in his first two seasons but wouldn't break out of his shell until the 1969–70 season.

While Orr was definitely not the first defence-man to rush into the offensive zone with the puck, he was the first to use his skills to such a devas-tating degree. Many teams were frustrated at his non-traditional approach to the defensive position and had a hard time containing him in one area of the rink. The Boston Garden crowd always held their breath just before the moment Orr broke out from behind the net and rushed to the other end untouched to score a goal or make a beautiful pass. By combining the rushing defensive talents of Orr with the solid offensive finishing touch of Phil Esposito, Boston head coach Harry Sinden had created one of the most effective two-way teams in the NHL at the time. Orr ended the regular season with a record-breaking 120 points in one season, and he was the first-ever defence-man to win a scoring title.

The next season Orr improved his season totals (despite the nagging knee injury that plagued him throughout his entire career) collecting the most points ever by a defenceman in one season with 139 total. The only defenceman to come close was Paul Coffey, who ended the 1986 season with 138 points when he played for the Edmonton Oilers.

With each passing year, Orr's knees deteriorated to the point where he could no longer effectively play his position and score those end-to-end goals that made him famous in Boston. After just nine full seasons of professional hockey, Orr was forced to retire from the game he loved at the young age of 31. One can only guess as to what his career would have looked like if he had not been plagued with the recurrent knee injuries; nonetheless, he remains one of the best players to have stood on the blue line.

First Death on NHL Ice: Bill Masterson

Bill Masterton only played 38 games in the National Hockey League, but his legacy would last forever. The Montréal Canadiens originally owned Bill Masterton's hockey rights but when, during the 1967 league expansion, they traded him to the Minnesota North Stars franchise for the start of the 1967-68 season. The tough centre's NHL career started off well when he scored the franchise's first goal on October 11, 1967. He wasn't one of the high-scoring forwards in the league, but his focus and dedication on the ice made him a perfect asset for the growth of a new franchise. It looked like he was headed for a long, successful career until the night of January 13, 1968, when the North Stars faced off against the Oakland Seals.

The game was going along smoothly, with both teams battling hard and getting equal chances on net. The North Stars started a rush up ice with Masterton leading the way, but as he came to the Seals blue line, the puck slipped off his stick and passed in between the two defencemen. As Masterton rushed in between them to go for a breakaway, they collided awkwardly sending the helmetless Masterton flying into the air. He lost his balance and struck his head on the ice. The play was stopped immediately as medics hurried out on the ice to tend to Masterton. He was rushed to hospital, but the damage to his brain was so severe and the swelling could not be controlled. He eventually succumbed to his injuries and died in the hospital two days later.

His career was short lived, but his passion for the game lived on when the NHL created the Bill Masterton Trophy the next year to be awarded to the player who best displays the qualities of perseverance, sportsmanship and dedication to the game of hockey. The first winner of the trophy was Claude Provost of the Montréal Canadiens.

First Defenceman to Play on a Broken Leg

It is with pride that hockey aficionados, especially Don Cherry, love to talk about how the game athletes are the toughest athletes in professional sports. Although there have been tough guys before him no player better exemplifies that spirit of manly manliness than Saskatchewan-born Toronto Maple Leaf defenceman Bob Baun.

A solid defenceman throughout his tenure in the NHL (1956-73), Baun never scored more than eight goals in one season but always remained a solid presence on the blue line. He was never the type of player that would come through in a clutch, but he was always reliable and played the game with intelligence. He won four Stanley Cups with the Toronto Maple Leafs, but the highlight of his individual career came in 1964 when the Leafs faced off against the Detroit Red Wings in the Stanley Cup finals and Baun got to play the hero.

It was a tough series, and after five games, the Red Wings held onto the series leading three game to two. The Leafs had the difficult task of having to win the next two games if they were going to bring the Cup back to Toronto for a third straight year. In Detroit for game six, the Leafs were battling hard to stay in the game with the score tied up at three. Gordie Howe was the Wings main offensive threat, and every time he stepped onto the ice, Maple Leafs head coach Punch Imlach put Baun on the ice to ensure he had a solid d-man to battle Howe in the corners. Howe managed to pick up the puck and began making his way toward the Toronto net, and just like Imlach had planned, Baun placed himself directly in front of the Wings superstar. But instead of trying to get around the tough Leafs defenceman, Howe decided to blast a shot off. Instead of finding the goaltender, the shot found its way onto the small unpadded area between the skate boot and the shin guard of Baun's leg.

"I heard a boom like a cannon. It was the bone cracking," said Baun after the incident.

Trying to stay in his position as the Red Wings pressed into the zone, Baun tried putting some weight on his leg but fell to the ice in obvious pain. The referee whistled the play dead and called for the trainers to attend to the fallen player. Baun was carried off the ice on a stretcher and into the Leafs dressing room where his injured leg was taped and frozen to numb the pain. Imlach knew that no player, no matter how tough, could come back from an injury like that, and he was forced to juggle his line to fill in the hole left by Baun.

Inside the dressing room Baun did not even think for one moment of taking himself out of the game. The team doctor tried to explain to him that his leg was too seriously injured to get back into the game, but Baun would hear nothing of it and told the doctor to patch him up because he was going back out. The Leafs had managed to contain the Red Wings in the third, sending the game into overtime. Baun knew he could not let his team down. Imlach and the rest of the Leafs could hardly believe their eyes as Baun came out of the dressing room and took his place on the bench for the start of overtime. Imlach wasn't sure if the Leafs defenceman could make it through the period but Baun nodded to the coach that he was ready, and when play got underway, Imlach sent him out onto the ice. It proved to be a great decision.

It wasn't the prettiest of goals, but Baun did not complain. After intercepting a Red Wings pass, Baun fired the puck into the Wings' zone. On the way in, it hit a defenceman's stick and bounced past the goaltender, winning the game for the Leafs and sending the series to game seven in Toronto.

After the game, Baun was noticeably wincing in pain but he refused to admit that he should be kept out of the line-up for game seven. He avoided team physicians so that he would not have to undergo an x-ray on his leg, knowing full well that his leg could be broken. His teammates knew something was wrong with him as he limped around the Leafs dressing before the start of game seven, but none of them said anything for fear of drawing attention to his condition and getting him removed from the line-up. He was the reason the Leafs were in game seven, and they felt he deserved the right to play.

Despite the obvious pain and the risk to his future NHL career, Baun suited up for game seven and played his regular shifts with the same intensity and physicality that he was known for. With his help, the Leafs won game seven 4–0 before the hometown crowd and took home their third straight Stanley Cup.

After the celebrations died down, Baun finally agreed to an x-ray. The film confirmed what he already knew—he had played two games with a broken shinbone. Explaining his ability to play despite the pain of a broken leg, Baun later said, "I guess it was my pain tolerance and the mental ability to block things out."

After the story got out, coaches around the league were heard to say to their injured players, "If Baun can play on a broken leg, what's your excuse?"

First Deaf Hockey Player

Over the years the NHL has seen many remarkable achievements by its players and the people that surround them, but no one had ever seen the likes of Jim Kyte when he joined the league in 1983 as the only deaf hockey player to play for an NHL team.

Kyte was the perfect stay-at-home defenceman with his 6'5" frame and 210 pounds, he could clear any opponent out of his goaltender's crease. Legally deaf, his hearing did limit his performance on the ice at times but nothing that created any serious problems. Not able to hear the whistle on an offside or icing, Kyte often continued battling in the corner with a confused opponent. He did wear a hearing aid to help boost the little hearing that he did have, but with the noise in the arena, Kyte had to rely on his instincts most of the time.

"When I was in junior, one guy used to call me "Radio Shack" all the time," said Kyte, laughing off the ribbings from his teammates.

After several years with the Winnipeg Jets, Kyte spent several years bouncing around teams before settling with the San Jose Sharks and eventually retiring in 1996 after 13 successful years in the NHL.

First Player Banned from the NHL for Life

No it's not Marty McSorley, but the first NHL player to be banned from the league for life was the Boston Bruins Billy Coutu way back in 1927.

Coutu was never the best player in the NHL, but he was a solid defenceman who could be relied on when things got a little rough in the corners or in front of the net. He began his career with the Montréal Canadiens, was loaned out to the Hamilton Tigers for one season and then was eventually traded to the Boston Bruins at the start of the 1926-27 regular season.

The Bruins were still a relatively new franchise at that point but had improved drastically from their horrible inaugural season in which they won just eight games. The Bruins felt that by acquiring tough veteran players like Coutu and Eddie Shore, they could substitute a level of skill for a physical presence on the ice that would intimidate their opponents—a strategy that many teams had tried and that the Bruins found necessary to help their young team.

Coutu was nearing the end of his career but felt this season with the Bruins was his chance for a second career. The Montréal Canadiens were headed away from the Coutu tough physical play to a faster game, but the Bruins were looking for a guy with his, shall we say, "talents," and Coutu was eager to deliver. But Coutu got his career with the Bruins off on a bad note when, during his first practice with the team, he took offence to some good-natured ribbing from his defensive partner Eddie Shore and then preceded to body-slam him into the ice, severing part of Shore's ear in the process.

Coutu and Shore would mend their ways and lead the Bruins defensive core to second place in the division and more importantly a spot in the playoffs for the first time in franchise history.

Coutu had passed through the regular season racking up his fair share of fights and penalties, but had done nothing out of the ordinary that would receive extra attention. But the playoffs are a new season, and Coutu had one surprise left in him before the year was over.

After making it through the opening rounds against the Chicago Black Hawks and the New

York Rangers, Boston made it into the finals against the Ottawa Senators. The Senators were an equally rough team that relied on their physical presence and the solid goaltending of Alex Connell rather than a strict offensive-oriented style. It had all the hallmarks of a good physical Stanley Cup series.

The series was an extremely tight, defensive affair with lots of physical play. It was the perfect series for Coutu, and he was hitting Senators left and right every time he stepped onto the ice. In game four of the series, Coutu's physical game got a bit out of hand. Boston Bruins manager Art Ross was famous for his need-to-win attitude. Down 3-1 in the dying moments of game four and with the Stanley Cup on the line, Ross needed an edge, something to get his team back in the game. His idea was simple. He had Coutu start a brawl. It was not a difficult task to accomplish. Coutu simply picked a player and started a fight, and soon both benches cleared. During the altercation, Coutu ended up punching referee Jerry Laflamme in the face. Punching a player repeatedly in the face is one thing, but hitting the referee is taboo. After the players were separated and the Senators finished off the Bruins to win the Cup, Coutu was brought before league president Frank Calder and was suspended from the NHL for life, becoming the first player to receive the dishonour.

Chapter Five

Coaches and Referees

First Coach to Become a Cultural Icon

DON CHERRY. The name now speaks for itself, but the high collared, loud-mouthed hockey icon that Canadians have come to love and hate with equal passion has become more than just a guy who talks hockey every Saturday on television, he has become a Canadian icon.

A high school dropout from Kingston, Ontario, Cherry like many other young Canadian boys sought his fame and fortune as a hockey player. Not blessed with any natural talent but making up for it with sheer will, Cherry spent most of his playing career bouncing around in the American Hockey League. He was a decent defenceman but there were countless other more talented players. However, Cherry never quit dreaming of making into the big leagues. He got his chance with the Boston Bruins in 1954-55 when he was called up to replace an injured player in the playoffs. It would be his only taste of the big leagues. But after 16 years of bouncing around from city to city moving his young family more than 50 times, he decided to hang up his skates in 1970. He returned briefly in 1971 to play for the Rochester Americans. Not long after, he was hired on as a replacement for the club's head coach and he began a new chapter in his hockey career.

Finally finding the right fit, Cherry spent three years behind the bench in Rochester before being promoted to the head coach position of his old team, the Boston Bruins, in 1974. Cherry was a passionate coach who was never afraid to chew out a player for underperforming or yell at a ref for a bad call. His antics behind the bench made him a fan favourite in Boston and of his players. He led the Bruins to four first place division titles in a row, but never could bring a Stanley Cup back to Boston. The final straw for Bruins management came during the 1979 playoff semi-finals versus the Montréal Canadiens. The Bruins had managed to force a deciding game seven against the Canadiens and looked poised to upset Montréal. Late into the third period of game seven the Canadiens were down 4-3, and the Bruins were just about to start celebrating their upset when the referee caught Boston with one too many players on the ice. When the

Bruins were assessed a two-minute bench minor, Cherry famously stood on the bench and mockingly gestured to the referees. The Canadiens' Guy Lafleur scored the tying goal, and the Canadiens went on to win the series and eventually their fourth straight Stanley Cup. After the play-offs, Cherry was dismissed as head coach of the Bruins despite having a record of 231 wins, 105 losses and 64 ties. He would go on to coach the Colorado Rockies for one unsuccessful season, before one appearance on the CBC's *Hockey Night in Canada* changed his life forever.

In 1980 Cherry appeared in a segment with host Dave Hodge for an interview. CBC officials happened to be watching and liked the passion and energy that Cherry brought to the television screen. They created a platform called *Coach's Corner* for the opinionated former coach to reach the masses. Paired up with host Ron Maclean, Cherry's show was an instant success as Cherry voiced his opinion on every matter related and unrelated to hockey. From the Canadian military to French and European players his commentaries court both positive and negative responses on a weekly basis. But love him or hate him, he quickly became a staple of Saturday night hockey all across the country. No *Hockey Night in Canada* broadcast is complete without a word and thumbs up from Don Cherry, and Canadians continue to tune into his show to hear his latest word on the game and life.

Although never a gifted hockey player and having remained a coach for a few seasons Cherry has worked his way into hockey consciousness with his bombastic style and incredible fashion sense. Canadians seem to connect with something in Cherry's to-the-point style where in a recent survey of the greatest Canadians in the history of this young country Don Cherry was named seventh greatest Canadian, above Wayne Gretzky, Alexander Graham Bell and General Romeo Dallaire. Not bad for a high school drop out from Kingston. Atta boy, Don!

First Coach to Play in Goal: Lester Patrick

Whenever sports stories are told about an amazing achievement or famous player, they tend to get romanticized and glorified to the point where the people involved become somewhat larger than the actual truth of the story. But when the story of the 1928 Stanley Cup finals between the New York Rangers and the Montréal Maroons is recounted, the truth is, in this case, stranger than fiction.

The 1927-28 season saw the Montréal Canadiens and the Montréal Maroons atop the NHL standings and on the score sheet. The Canadiens, with players like Howie Morenz and Aurel Joliat finishing first and second in scoring were easy favourites to take home the cup, but the Maroons with scoring talent like Nels Stewart who had scored 27 goals during the season were no slouches either. In the American division, the New York Rangers were edged out by the Boston Bruins during the regular season but bounced back for the playoffs in the quarter and semi-finals to beat the Pittsburgh Pirates and the Bruins. The Rangers then advanced to the Stanley Cup finals to face off against a tough Maroons squad that had just defeated the high-scoring Montréal Canadiens in a nail biter of a series.

The Rangers, coached by hockey legend Lester Patrick, had a powerful scoring line-up with players like Bun Cook, Frank Boucher and Bill Cook, which when added to a solid defensive core with Ivan "Ching" Johnson (weighing in at 210 pounds he was a formidable obstacle in front of the net) and the goaltending of Lorne Chabot, the Rangers had a team that could match the offensive and break the defensive talents of the Maroons as long as every player remained healthy.

Before things could even get started, the Rangers were handed their first obstacle on their road to the Cup. Madison Square Garden, it seems, was a popular venue, and with the circus in town at the time of the playoffs, the Rangers were forced to find a new arena for their home games seeing that the circus was the bigger draw. As general manager and head coach, Lester Patrick had the option of playing their home games in Boston or Detroit but instead he choose the larger ice surface of the Montréal Forum because it favoured his quick skaters over the slower more defence-oriented Maroons.

Game one did not start out the way Patrick was hoping. The Maroons potted goals in the second and third periods, while Montréal netminder Clint Benedict stopped every single shot that came his way for the 2-0 victory before the Maroons hometown crowd. Going into the second game Patrick knew his team would have to get men in front of Benedict because, if he saw the puck coming, there was no way he was going to miss the save. Benedict had only allowed on average a goal per game in the playoffs and wasn't about to start letting the Rangers ruin his record.

For the second game, Patrick knew his team had to come out playing hard. The Maroons had excellent scoring power, but it was the defence and the goaltending of Clint Benedict that the Rangers needed to solve in order to win the next game.

With the usual fanfare, the game got underway, and Patrick kept his best defensive line on the ice against the Nels Stewart line hoping to keep the game close for the Rangers scoring line to do their job. All was going according to plan when fate intervened and made this series, and this game in particular, one to remember.

At just the four-minute mark of the first period Maroons star Nels Stewart broke into the Rangers zone and let loose a cannon of a shot that struck Rangers goaltender Lorne Chabot just above the eye. Chabot hit the ice unconscious and bleeding profusely from his wound. As paramedics put Chabot onto a stretcher and rushed him to the hospital, Patrick was left to deal with the fact that he had no goaltender to replace Chabot with for the rest of the game.

At a time in the league when teams only dressed one goaltender, Patrick was faced with the dilemma of replacing Chabot with a player or forfeiting the game. Patrick knew that Ottawa Senators goaltender Alec Connell was attending the game and immediately sent a request to the Maroons bench requesting that the Rangers use Connell in place of Chabot since they had no back up goaltender. Maroons manager Eddie Girard fired back refusing to allow Connell or any other person not under contract with the Rangers to replace Chabot in goal.

He politely denied Patrick's request and ended with, "If you need a goalkeeper, why the hell doesn't Lester play?"

Girard wasn't born yesterday. Connell was one of the best goaltenders in the league, posting 15 shutouts during the regular season and only allowing just over one goal per game with a 1.24 average. Goals were hard enough to come by with Chabot in nets, so adding one of the best shutout goaltenders into a Stanley Cup game would be a foolish move on Girard's part.

Patrick was left with very few options. He either had to dress one of his forwards or forfeit the game and hand the Maroons the easy win. With one last defiant glare at the Maroons bench, Patrick made the decision that he thought he would never have to make again and would go down in history as one of the most exciting moments in hockey.

With great hesitation, Patrick started putting on Chabot's sweaty pads. At the age of 44, Lester Patrick, coach and manager of the New York Rangers, was going to play in goal during a Stanley Cup game. Once the Rangers realized what Patrick was doing, they all tried to talk him out of it, but the stubborn, old hockey veteran could not be talk out of playing. When he was much younger and in better shape he had taken up the position in between the posts when his team had needed him, but now his movements weren't the same, and many on the Rangers bench wondered if the old Silver Fox was going to make it through the game let alone stop any shots.

To the shock of everyone in the stands and especially Eddie Girard on the Maroons bench, Patrick skated out onto the ice and took his position. After a couple of stretches and a few practice shots, the referees readied for the face-off. Playing with a renewed sense of purpose, the Rangers defence took it upon themselves to keep the Maroons as far away from their coach as possible. Yet, no matter how hard they tried the Maroons' offence still managed to get a few shots on net, but Patrick managed to close out the first and second period with the score still tied at 0 apiece.

One can only guess now at what was said in between periods in the Rangers dressing room, but it seemed to work as the Rangers came out wanting to win the game for their coach who had risked everything to keep them in the game. Patrick got the response he wanted from his players/teammates when Bill Cook scored after only 20 seconds into the third period. The Maroons, however, were not finished and continued to press into the Rangers zone and cracking off a few shots at the aging goaltender. Nels Stewart finally put the puck behind Patrick at 14:20 of the third period to tie up the game and send it into overtime—undoubtedly much to the dismay of a tired-looking Rangers goaltender.

For the overtime period, the Rangers redoubled their efforts so that their coach's sacrifice would not have to be in vain. They could see Patrick's tired eyes and wanted to end the game as fast as they could. It took just seven minutes before Frank Boucher split the Montréal defence, turned Benedict inside out and scored the game-winning goal. At the very moment the goal hit the back of the net, Patrick let out a great sigh of relief and braced himself for the mob of Rangers flying off the bench to congratulate him. In the end, Patrick had stopped 17 of 18 shots on goal, not a bad effort for 44-year-old coach. For the next game, Patrick hung up his pads and any illusions of playing again and called up a minor league goalie to replace Chabot. Although they lost that game, Chabot would return to win game four and five to lead the Rangers to their first-ever Stanley Cup Championship.

Despite his illustrious career as a player and a coach, Lester Patrick, the Silver Fox, will always be remembered as the 44-year-old coach who came off the bench, played in goal and won a Stanley Cup game.

First Coach to Pull Goalie for an Extra Attacker

While some historians refer to Chicago Black Hawks head coach Paul Thompson as the first coach to pull his goalie in favour of an extra attacker in a 1941 game versus the Boston Bruins, the strategy was actually used 10 years early by Boston Bruins head coach Art Ross in a 1-0 loss versus the Canadiens on March 26, 1931, in game two of the Stanley Cup semi-finals.

First Coach to Change on the Fly

Hard to imagine a game today in which players had to change lines at the whistle with players now logging 30 to 45 second shifts, but before 1925, it was normal for a player to be on the ice for a minute or longer, waiting for a stoppage in play before they could get off the ice.

The first coach to be credited with changing lines while the play was still in progress was the Victoria Cougars head coach Lester Patrick of the Western Canadian Hockey League in the Stanley Cup finals against the Montréal Canadiens.

First Referee

Fred Waghorne was one of the game's greatest innovators. During a time when the game had no official set of rules, Waghorne's quick on-ice decisions often became the governing laws of hockey that still remain to this day. Among his many contributions to the game:

- Waghorne was the first referee to use a whistle during a game.

- He was the first referee to use the face-off during a game where the referee dropped the puck from a few feet up rather than playing it directly on the ice. This limited the players' sticks coming into contact with the referees shins and ankles.

- He came up with the rule that if half a broken puck entered the net, no goal was counted. This rule led to the development of one-piece pucks.

- He had the idea of using a whistle instead of the customary cowbell to stop play when fans started bringing their own cowbells to game to disrupt play.

In his career he refereed over 2400 hockey games and was elected into the Hockey Hall of Fame in the builder category in 1961. But after his retirement from officiating he continued to remain close to the game, establishing the Beaches Hockey League, which eventually became the Greater Toronto Hockey League. He died in 1956 at the age of 90.

Chapter Six

Team Firsts

First Hockey Team to Wear the Swastika

Throughout the majority of human history the swastika was known by many cultures as a symbol for good luck, peace and good fortune. It wasn't until Adolf Hitler and his brutal Nazi regime that the swastika became a symbol of extreme hatred and violence. So it seemed a perfectly normal symbol and name for the hockey team from Windsor to use when they formed a new team in 1905. The Windsor Swastikas proudly displayed the symbol on their jerseys until 1916 and were known in the region as one of the top-notch clubs with an exciting brand of fast, high-scoring hockey.

The First Dynasty

Canada's capital city was a centre for hockey long before Lord Stanley donated his Stanley Cup in 1893. The larger cities in the east had already established a tradition of competition in games of hockey at winter carnivals and festivals. They wanted to claim bragging rights to the title of the best hockey players in the country. Quickly, the hockey games became major social events that attracted the high society crowd to the new thrilling game. Canada's governor at the time, the Right Honourable Sir Frederick Arthur Stanley—commonly referred to as Lord Stanley—was a passionate supporter of the game and particularly of the Ottawa Club that his son Arthur played for regularly. It was for this love of the game and his hope to see his son succeed that he created a Challenge Cup for which the best teams in Canada could compete.

The Montréal Amateur Athletic Association was awarded the Cup without having to play for it since they had won the regular season championship in the Amateur Hockey Association. But competing at this time was a team from Ottawa that would rise to prominence. By 1903 the Ottawa Hockey Club found the right combination of players that would see them finally able to challenge the domination of the Cup by the Montréal-based teams.

Ottawa's line-up was one of the best hockey had ever seen, with players such as Harvey Pulford, Harry Westwick, the Gilmour brothers Bill,

Dave and Shuddy, and goaltender Bouse Hutton. But the player that made the biggest difference to the success of the team had to be the forward Frank McGee.

Frank McGee had earned quite a name for himself in the Ottawa city leagues as a formidable opponent on the ice and in the many other sports in which he participated. But hockey was what he excelled at, and it was on the ice that he would create his legend. In the first game of that season on January 17, 1903, against the defending Stanley Cup champion Montréal AAA, McGee's puck-handling abilities and speed led him to score 2 goals in a 7-1 victory. Just a few weeks later, Ottawa fans got to see the full scope of McGee's talent in a game against the Montréal Victorias. McGee was on the ice for most of the game and seemed to always have the puck on the end of his stick. After scoring one goal, McGee received a round of polite applause from the crowd, but after his second, third, fourth and fifth goals, the crowd cheered loudly. Word of McGee's exploits spread around the league, and soon he was attracting more and more fans to the game. After playing in just six of the eight regular-season games, McGee had scored 14 goals and helped his Ottawa club to a first-place tie with the Montréal Victorias. Ottawa and Montréal met in a two-game total-goal series to decide who would take home the Stanley Cup. The previous owners of the Cup, the Montréal AAA, failed to finish the CAHL regular season with enough points, which put the Cup up for grabs to the winner of the championship game. In the first game of the series, the two teams battled to a 1-1 tie but Ottawa turned on the offensive switch in the second game—despite the layer of water that covered the ice—and won the game by a score of 8-0. The victory over the Victorias gave the Ottawa Hockey Club their first Stanley Cup championship and earned them a new name.

After the game, as the team members were celebrating their first Stanley Cup, an unknown supporter showed up with a gift for each of the players to show his gratitude—a silver nugget. As word began to spread of the generous gift, Ottawa became known as the Silver Seven (silver because of the nuggets and seven because of the old rule that had an extra player on the ice, called a rover).

A short time later, the Silver Seven had to defend their championship against the Rat Portage Thistles on March 12, 1903. In those days, it was the custom that the defending Stanley Cup champion could be challenged at any time. Ottawa had little trouble against the Rat Portage team in the two-game series, winning by scores of 6-2 and 4-2. Frank McGee was once again the standout player on the Silver Seven, scoring seven goals in the series.

During the regular season he was outstanding, but during the Stanley Cup games he was simply unstoppable. But Ottawa was not able to rest after successfully defending their Stanley Cup championship against Rat Portage (now known as the town of Kenora). Those early victories and the presence of Frank McGee had quickly earned Ottawa a reputation as one of the best teams in hockey, and it would take a Herculean effort to take away the championship from the Silver Seven.

In the first challenge of 1904, from the Winnipeg Rowing Club team, Ottawa established itself as one of the greatest scoring teams in hockey history. The sports pundits of the times predicted it as an easy victory for the Silver Seven, and in the first game it seemed like the Winnipeg team had no hope, losing the game 9-1. But Winnipeg would not be intimidated by the powerful Ottawa offence and hit back with a big 6-2 victory, holding the great McGee to no goals. Winnipeg knew that in order to stop the Ottawa juggernaut, they would need to play a very physical game.

For the third game of the series, bodies banged together in the corners, sticks flew and blood stains dotted the ice, but neither team managed to score during the first 45 minutes of the game.

So after nearly killing each other for the majority of the game, the Winnipeg players ran out of energy and could not stop Ottawa from putting two goals by their goaltender for a 2-0 victory and the right to hold onto the Cup. It was a tough series, but the Silver Seven proved to be the toughest team of the day. One writer for the *Winnipeg Free Press* described the series afterward:

> *Hospital cases of rowing Club: P. Brown, lame; C. Richards, face swollen, leg hurt; C. Bennest, thumb broken, badly bruised; W. Breen, bruised and broken up; J. Hall, cut on head; D. Kirby, cut on head; W. Bawlf, cut and bruised. Seven out of nine injured; two forced to retire from game; three forced to remain in bed after the game; one out of hockey for season.*

> *It is an open secret that if any team is to beat Ottawa at home in any sport, they must be at least a third stronger.*

Just a few weeks after that brutal series Ottawa was challenged again and turned away the Toronto Marlboros to retain the title. In March 1904, the Montréal Wanderers tried to take the Cup in another challenge series, and Ottawa again beat them back. Then it was the Brandon Wheat Kings and the Dawson City Nuggets in 1905, before Ottawa finally lost the Cup to the Montréal Wanderers in 1906. Led by the incredible

Frank McGee, the Ottawa Silver Seven are the shin-
ning example of what it took to achieve a dynasty
in the sport of hockey—scoring, goaltending and
sheer grit.

First Game of the Montréal Canadiens

When professional hockey was first established
in North America, it was for a long time largely
the domain of the upper class Anglophones.
French Canadians had fallen in love with the
game along with the rest of the country but lacked
a team to represent their unique contribution to
the game.

Since the first hockey leagues were formed,
Montréal had several teams competing for fans
and the Stanley Cup, but those franchises, including the Montréal Amateur Athletic Association,
the Montréal Wanderers, the Montréal Shamrocks
and the Montréal Victorias, were run by and
mostly populated with Anglophones.

Francophones were long considered second-
class citizens and did not have the means to
organize a professional team. There were local
games in small communities, but no official
team to call their own and cheer for. Professional
hockey was for the old boys club, and they didn't
want any new members, especially French ones.
So when a young, rich Anglophone named

J. Ambrose O'Brien arrived on the scene and wanted to form a team consisting of mainly French athletes and run by French coaches and managers, he met with some stiff opposition from the established teams right from the start. But O'Brien was persistent, and he waited for the right opportunity to move forward.

O'Brien had heard through his contacts that a rift was developing in the Eastern Canadian Hockey Association (ECHA) between owners. This was the chance he needed to get his Montréal franchise.

The Montréal Wanderers wanted the right to play home games in their own building, the Jubilee Rink, in the eastern part of the city, but the other teams in the league wanted to play in the larger more profitable Westmount Arena. Wanderers owner P.J. Doran, who just happened to own the Jubilee Rink, refused to cooperate and was summarily kicked out of the ECHA. O'Brien attended the ECHA's next meeting in hopes of taking the spot vacated by the Wanderers, but he was laughed out of the room for the very idea of bringing another hockey team to a city that was already overrun with hockey teams. And it was a French team on top of it all!

At that same meeting was a man named Jimmy Gardner, an executive officer for the

Wanderers who had hoped to make the ECHA members rethink their decision to remove his team from the new season. Obviously failing in his attempt to sway the members, he stormed out of the meeting and sat down beside O'Brien. The two began to talk, and they easily found common ground in their hatred of the ECHA members. Garder suggested the best way they could get revenge was to set up their own hockey league. On December 4, 1909, a meeting was called in room 129 of Montréal's Windsor Hotel to finalize the formation of a new league, called the National Hockey Association (NHA).

It was announced at the meeting that the new franchises in the league had been awarded to five clubs: the Montréal Wanderers, the Cobalt Silver Kings, Haileybury and the Renfrew Creamery Kings, and the new yet unnamed Montréal team. Naming the new team, however, proved to be a rather easy affair. Since it was to be made up of mainly French Canadian players, it was simply called "le Club de Hockey Canadien, or the Montréal Canadiens.

Jack Laviolette, who had many connections in the Francophone hockey world, was given the task of assembling the players for the first game of the Montréal Canadiens on January 5, 1910, at the Jubilee Rink against the Cobalt

Silver Kings. Once the new team was firmly established and the new league was deemed viable, the management of the Canadiens as a business was to be handed over entirely to French Canadians.

In less than a month, Laviolette had assembled a competitive team. It had two star players in Didier Pitre and Newsy Lalonde, along with Joe Cattarinich, Ed Decary, Arthur Bernier, Georges Poulin, Ed Chapleau, Ed Millaire, Noss Chartrand and Richard Duckett. With the team in place, the Canadiens were ready to hit the ice for their first game.

More than 3000 spectators pushed their way into Jubilee Rink to witness the Canadiens' first NHA game. Through the heavy layer of cigarette smoke that filled the arena, to the raucous applause of the fans, the Canadiens made their first public appearance wearing blue jerseys bearing a white stripe running down their shoulders and across their chests and a large white "C" on the front. White pants and red socks finished off the iconic bleu, blanc and rouge that the Canadiens have become known for.

Only 17 minutes into the game, Newsy Lalonde scored the first goal in the Montréal Canadiens history and the first for the NHA, as well. Skinner Poulin put in another goal to power the

Canadiens ahead 2-0, and before the period was over (there were just two 30-minute periods with a 10-minute break in those days), Newsy Lalonde got the crowd on their feet with a beautiful end-to-end rush through the entire opposing team to score the Canadiens' third goal. During the second period, the Cobalt Kings came back in the game, but each time they scored, the Canadiens managed to return the favour—much to the delight of their new fans. By the end of the game, the score was tied 6-6 in overtime. In just over five minutes, Canadiens forward Skinner Poulin scored the winning goal.

The next day, the *Montréal Gazette* described the Canadiens' victory: "The winning of the match was the signal for a demonstration that recalled old Stanley Cup struggles. The rink was filled with a gathering that gave the Canadiens as loyal support as any hockey team ever received in Montréal."

The team was an instant success in the city as people spread the word of the fast-paced, skilful hockey played by the Francophone team. Although the Canadiens won only two games that season, they had firmly established a place in the hearts and minds of the people of Montréal.

After just one year in existence, the owners of the Montréal Canadiens ran into some legal trouble from George Kennedy, who owned the

French Canadien hockey team in Montréal's east end called Club Athlétique Canadien. Kennedy wanted to get his hands on an NHA franchise and threatened to go to court to stop the league from using the name Canadiens since he had been operating his team before the NHA was formed. Not wanting to have to go to court and suffer bad press, Kennedy was given the Haileybury Hockey Club franchise to operate as the Canadiens while J. Ambrose O'Brien withdrew the 1909-10 Canadiens from the league. But this change in ownership did nothing to stop the excitement and tension that they Canadiens brought to Montréal.

In what would become a common complaint of the Canadiens organization over the years, Kennedy often complained that the league and the referees were doing everything in their power to make sure that the French team from Montréal lost their games. After a 5-4 loss against the Wanderers at the Westmount Arena, Kennedy said loudly and clearly so the newspapermen could hear that he wanted to have a French referee shadow the English ones at the rest of the Canadiens' games to make sure his team wasn't being cheated. Kennedy endeared himself to the French population of Montréal even more when he publicly threatened to sue the Canadian Pacific Railway because the Canadiens' equipment did not arrive in time for their game in Renfrew.

Although Kennedy was a Montréaler and supporter of the French team in Montréal, he strangely enough had the Canadiens jersey changed in favour of a solid red jersey with a large green maple leaf on the chest and an ornate "C" in the middle of the leaf. Hard to imagine a Montréal Canadiens sweater with a Maple Leaf on it but it did not last long and was changed the following season.

First Team to Win 10 Straight Playoff Victories

With more teams joining the league and the competition for Lord Stanley's Cup becoming longer and more difficult, the time of the dynasty had long since passed, and teams now had to battle a larger pool of players, all with only one purpose in mind. The 1992-93 season was a time of major change in the National Hockey League as it welcomed two new teams—the Tampa Bay Lighting and the Ottawa Senators—decommissioned the league president in favour of a commissioner and expanded the league season by four games to accommodate the new teams—all this highlighted by the celebration of the 100th anniversary of Lord Stanley's Cup.

The regular season ended with the champion Pittsburgh Penguins on top of the league with 119 points, but with three new teams in the league, other stronger clubs feasted on the new franchises, running up their point totals to where seven teams enjoyed 100-plus point seasons. Going into the playoffs, it was expected that the Pittsburgh Penguins, Chicago Black Hawks, Detroit Red Wings, Boston Bruins and Québec Nordiques would all advance to the second round. But expectations are one thing and reality is another. The playoffs wipe the slate clean for the teams that finish with mediocre records and give them a chance in what is commonly referred to as the "second season," in which hard work, heart and a little luck can get any team into the finals. The first round of the playoffs were cruel to the "stronger" teams, as all but the Penguins were eliminated, leaving the Stanley Cup open to all the underdogs.

In the province of Québec, a classic battle between two archrivals renewed itself for one last time as the Canadiens and the Nordiques battled for the right to advance to the next round. The series got underway before a sea of blue and white at the Colisée in Québec City, and the teams battled to a 2-2 tie by the end of the third period, much to the nervous delight of the Nordiques fans. Game one ended with a goal from Scott Young, giving the Nordiques the advantage in the series to the relief of the capacity crowd. The Nordiques completely dominated the Canadiens in game two, making Patrick Roy look like a rookie as they pumped four goals past the flustered netminder. After the second loss, Canadiens coach Jacques Demers was asked by the media if he was going to replace Patrick in nets for game three, but the coach stood by his veteran goaltender, knowing that when the pressure was on, Roy would always perform.

The Canadiens came back in game three on the strength of Patrick Roy's return to form in goal and the start of a record playoff overtime win record, taking game three 2-1 in OT off a goal from Vincent Damphousse. The rest of the series belonged to the Canadiens as Patrick Roy shut down the Nordiques' snipers, and the Canadiens' rookies stepped up and scored the much-needed goals that would propel them into the next round of the Cup playoffs against the Buffalo Sabres.

Always with a flare for the dramatic during the playoffs, the Canadiens won game one against the Sabres in Montréal 4-3 in regulation time, and then won the next three games by the exact same score, though all the games were won in overtime. This was the first time since the 1970 Detroit-Chicago series that a playoff series had ended with the same score in every game. Montréal's overtime magic continued into the Prince of Wales finals against the New York

Islanders, with two more overtime wins to bring their streak to seven straight. With their strong overtime wins, the Canadiens took a 3-0 lead in the series and only faltered in game four, losing 4-1 before finishing off the tired Islanders with a 5-2 victory. This was the first time back in the finals for Montréal since they had lost to the Calgary Flames in 1989. They wouldn't know who they were going to play for a couple of days, as the Toronto Maple Leafs and the Los Angeles Kings battled in one of the most entertaining series of the year for any fan of playoff hockey.

Toronto's path to the Campbell Conference finals was not an easy one. They came out of the first round of playoffs against Detroit with an overtime win in game seven, followed by a long, hard-fought series against the St. Louis Blues. They won that series in a slightly more convincing fashion with a 6-0 victory in game seven, but they were about to face their toughest challenge of the 1993 playoffs—Wayne Gretzky and a hot Los Angeles squad.

All of Canada was excited at the possibility of a Montréal versus Toronto Stanley Cup final. The two bitter rivals had not faced off against each other since the 1967 finals, and it would have been the perfect story to cap off the 100th anniversary of the Stanley Cup. But one player had a different ending in mind.

Wayne Gretzky hadn't been to the Stanley Cup finals since he'd left the Edmonton Oilers and joined the Los Angeles Kings organization. Toronto looked like they had the series in hand with an overtime win in game five to give them the 3-2 advantage in the series, but Los Angeles bounced back with a controversial overtime win to stay alive and force a seventh game. It was controversial because right before the goal, Gretzky had high-sticked Leafs forward Doug Gilmour, drawing blood. It should have been an automatic penalty whether it had been intentional or an accident, but the call was overlooked, and Gretzky ended up scoring the winning goal. Like it or not, the Leafs were going to a seventh and deciding game. In what Gretzky himself calls his greatest game, he scored a hat trick and added an assist to lead the Kings to their first-ever Cup final. This would be Montréal's 34th appearance in the Stanley Cup final.

The Kings looked like the team that wanted to win the Cup more in game one, taking it easily by a score of 4-1 on the back of Wayne Gretzky's goal and three assists. Montréal was not going to hand the Cup over to the Kings, and Patrick Roy kept his young team in the game with some spectacular saves in game two. But that still wasn't enough, as the Kings had a 2-1 lead with the third period ticking away. Facing a 2-0 series deficit, Montréal head coach Jacques Demers made a controversial call that changed the course of the series.

Acting on a tip from one of his players, Montréal head coach Jacques Demers made a risky call to have Marty McSorley's stick measured for an illegal curve. Demers nervously paced behind the Canadiens bench while officials measured the stick. The stick turned out to have an illegal curve, and McSorley was penalized for the remainder of regulation time for the infraction. Montréal defenceman Éric Desjardins scored the equalizer to send the game into overtime. It took just 51 seconds of overtime for Desjardins to score his third goal of the game, giving the Canadiens the much-needed victory and, better still, the momentum in the series.

After the game, Los Angeles Kings head coach Barry Melrose was obviously upset by Demers tactics. "I don't believe in winning that way."

Montréal, on the other hand, was flying high after their overtime win. "Without being cocky, when it comes to overtime, we just feel we can win," said Coach Jacques Demers after the Canadiens game two overtime win made it their eighth straight victory. The Canadiens managed another overtime victory on a goal by their big forward, John LeClair, in game three to take a 2-1 series lead. The Kings seemed to have lost all their energy after the heartbreaking overtime losses, as the Canadiens kept Gretzky from stealing the show with a great checking game and relied heavily on the goaltending of Patrick Roy. The Canadiens goaltender's confidence was so high that in overtime of game four, after he robbed Kings forward Tomas Sandstrom of a sure goal, he goaded the player further by winking at him.

It was do-or-die time for the Los Angeles Kings in game five at the Montréal

Forum. The Canadiens had not won the Cup on home ice since 1979, and the Forum that night was packed to capacity with an army of fans hoping to end the series at home. After the first period, it was obvious the Kings just didn't have what it took to mount a proper comeback, and they lost the final game by a score of 4-1. The Canadiens players launched their gloves in the air and swarmed around their star goaltender. Patrick Roy had proved once again that he was a clutch goaltender, and he took home the Conn Smythe Trophy for his efforts.

"I'm so proud of this team," said Demers after the win. "There were so many favourites, but we never stopped believing. We were like the boxer who didn't want to go down."

In the Los Angeles dressing room, things weren't as cheerful. "We're at a loss for words," said captain Wayne Gretzky.

It was the perfect ending to the National Hockey League's 75th anniversary, and the Stanley Cup's 100th that the league's most storied and most decorated team took home the Cup that year.

The First NHL Team to Go on Strike

During a time when the team's starting player almost stayed in for an entire game, any extra games added to the schedule would have exacted a heavy toll on the players physical condition. So when the league went from playing 24 games in 1923-24 to a 30-game schedule the following year, added two more franchises in Boston and in Montréal and expanded the playoff format to two rounds instead of one, players felt they should be paid accordingly. The players had a legitimate argument because all the extra revenue from the new teams and the expanded playoffs would be split evenly amongst the NHL owners, and the players would get none. Other teams had given their players bonuses, but the Hamilton Tigers ownership did not, so the players refused to play against their NHL finals opponents, the Montréal

Canadiens, until they were paid about $200 each. The league responded by threatening to fine each player $200 if they did not play in the NHL finals, but the Hamilton players decided they would rather quit the game than be taken advantage of. Montréal was declared NHL champion and went on to face the Victoria Cougars in the Stanley Cup finals, which they lost three games to one. That summer, the Hamilton Tigers franchise was sold to a group in New York, and they became the New York Americans the following season.

Canada's First Olympic Gold

In an official record of Canada's participation in the Winter Olympics it is written that the Great White Northern country won its first ice hockey medal in Chamonix, France in 1924, but technically Canada won its first-ever Olympic ice hockey gold at the 1920 Summer Olympics in Belgium!

The Winnipeg Falcons had just come off an incredible season in the Senior Amateur Hockey League winning the Allan Cup Championship. After their display of superior hockey skills, the International Olympic Committee asked them to join their fellow Canadian athletes at the 1920 Olympics in Antwerp, Belgium. It did seem a little strange that an ice hockey team was being invited to compete in the Summer Games, but they had also invited figure skaters, so it appeared that the IOC was pushing to open a new winter version of the Games.

With dreams of Olympic gold in their heads, the Canadian men's hockey team bulldozed their way through the competition beating the U.S., Sweden and Czechoslovakia by a combined score of 28-1.

Along with receiving their shiny new medals, the Canadian hockey team received an official piece of paper stating that they had indeed won the hockey gold medal of the first official Winter Olympic Games. The Winnipeg Falcons beamed with pride at the gold medals around their necks, knowing that they would go down history as winning in the first Winter Games. But years later, the IOC repealed their decision to name the 1920 Olympic Games as the first Winter Games and handed that honour to the 1924 Chamonix, France Winter Olympics.

At those 1924 Olympics, the Canadian hockey team won the gold medal again and was officially given the recognition as the first team to win Olympic hockey gold. It was only until many years later that the 1920 Winnipeg Falcons were recognized as official Olympic champions, although for the 1920 Summer Games.

First Stanley Cup in the Montréal Forum

Many people would say that the Montréal Canadiens were the first team to win a Stanley Cup in the legendary Montréal Forum, but they are forgetting about another Montréal team that existed from 1924 to 1938.

In the first few years of the National Hockey League, the Montréal Canadiens were the heart of the city, but they did not have a real home. For the inaugural season of the NHL, the Canadiens shared the Westmount Arena with the Montréal Wanderers, but when the building burnt to the ground in January of 1918, the Canadiens went to the 3250-seat Jubilee Arena on the east end of the city before settling in at the Mount Royal Arena at the corner of Mount Royal and St. Urbain. The Montréal Wanderers, without a home, folded operations and never returned. This was also the first time that English Montréal was without a professional level hockey team (the Canadiens represented the French side of the city).

There was interest in bringing back an English hockey team to Montréal, but without a home, a new franchise would never get off the ground. Realizing the need for a new home for English hockey, Senator Donat Raymond and hockey builder William Northey approached the man most able to help them get the funding needed to build a stadium to house the new team. Chairman of Canadian Pacific Railway Edward W. Beatty was sympathetic to the proposal of Raymond and Northey and quickly began gathering the funds needed from the wealthy people of Montréal to build a new stadium. By the spring of 1924, $406,000 had been raised to build a new home for English hockey in the city. When the 1924 NHL season began, Montréal Maroons had a brand new home dubbed the Montréal Forum.

Just one year after joining the NHL, the 1925-26 version of the Montréal Maroons became one of the league's top teams. With legendary players such as Nels Stewart, Babe Siebert and goaltender Clint Benedict, the Maroons eclipsed their Montréal counterparts who finished out that season in the basement of the league. The Maroons finished the season in second place just behind the powerful Ottawa Senators, but the regular season was just a formality. The playoffs are the true test of a team's grit, and the Maroons proved to be the better team. The Maroons dispatched the Pittsburgh Pirates in the NHL semi-finals and then did the same to the Ottawa Senators in the NHL finals.

Although the Maroons had defeated the Senators in the NHL finals, it did not mean they had won the Cup. That year was the last time

teams from other leagues could challenge the best
in the NHL for the right to be named Stanley Cup
Champion. The Victoria Cougars of the Western
Hockey League had won the Cup the previous
year over the Montréal Canadiens, and this year
they would return to defend their title against the
Maroons. But six goals by Nels Stewart and some
crafty goaltending by Clint Benedict put a stop to
the Cougars' quest for a second Cup. The Maroons
ended the series with a 2-0 victory in the Forum
to win the first Cup in the Montréal Forum.

First Cup to Be Cancelled Due to a Players' Strike

In 1994, NHL hockey fans got their first taste of
what it would be like to endure a winter with no
hockey when the NHL Players Association
(NHLPA) and NHL management could not resolve
a contract dispute and were forced to cut the season in half. Luckily for the fans, the two sides
finally came to an agreement and continued the
season at the halfway point, managing to get in
48 games before the start of the playoffs. Unfortunately, though, in their rush to save the season,
the two sides left certain areas in the players
contract unresolved—a ticking time bomb that
was very likely to bring about the same results
when the contract ran out 10 years later.

Fast-forward 10 years to the 2004-05 season, and the contract dispute reared its ugly head again. At stake was another season of NHL hockey and millions of dollars in lost revenue for the league, the players and the businesses that survive off professional hockey. The main issue of contention when it came down to it all was money. Owners said they didn't have enough and wanted to put a cap on spending. The players didn't believe the league was in such a bad state as the league said, and thus began months of passing blame. There were some hopeful moments throughout the dispute, but by January it was clear that neither side would budge, and that for the first time in National Hockey League history, an entire season as well as the playoffs was cancelled. It was the only time a season had been cancelled since the influenza epidemic of 1919 had called off the finals between the Montréal Canadiens and the Seattle Metropolitans.

For the first time, legions of fans were left for an entire winter with no hockey and were forced to reacquaint themselves with their loved ones on Saturday nights. Many people, instead of watching the game, took out their old skates and hit the local rinks, rediscovering the passion for the game that they had when they were kids.

After all the bickering and contract discussions, the NHLPA and league management finally came to an agreement on July 13, 2005, and hockey came back the next season. But the damage was done. Some NHL players retired, scoring records were interrupted and most importantly, the Stanley Cup was not awarded. Many people agreed with an initiative to have the Stanley Cup returned to its original purpose and given out to the best team in a challenge series. The league protested, saying that it had sole rights to the Cup, but finally capitulated before a court that if the NHL for some reason could not hand out the Cup to one of its teams, then the Cup would go to the team who best exhibited the skills and passion that Lord Stanley originally saw in the game of hockey. Only time will tell if this will come to pass.

The First Stanley Cup for Each Team

Montréal Canadiens

The Montréal Canadiens won their first Stanley Cup in 1916 when they belonged to the National Hockey Association. After the NHA folded to be replaced by the National Hockey League, it took the Canadiens several years before being able to hoist the silver cup again.

After a few seasons struggling behind more powerful teams like the Ottawa Senators, the Montréal Canadiens added a few key players to their line-up that brought them back to prominence. Canadiens general manager Leo Dandurand discovered unique talent languishing in a small-town league in Stratford, Ontario, before the start of the 1923 season. Dandurand received a call from a referee friend who had just witnessed a young man by the name of Howarth W. Morenz score nine goals in a playoff game for the Ontario Hockey Association. The referee told Dandurand to come to Stratford and sign this talent before any other team could. It took some convincing, but Howie Morenz joined the Canadiens for the start of the 1923-24 season and made an immediate impact on the team's fortunes.

Placed on a line with the Canadiens' top scorers, Aurel Joliat and Billy Boucher, Morenz and the Canadiens became one of the keague's best teams, finishing in second place to the dreaded Senators.

In the NHL finals, with the help of Morenz, the Canadiens easily defeated the Senators in a two-game total-goal series (the team with the most goals after two games advanced to the Stanley Cup finals). Morenz led the way scoring three of the team's five goals.

In the Stanley Cup finals, Montréal was forced to play against two western teams instead of one as had previously been done because Pacific Coast Hockey Association president Frank Patrick insisted that the NHL finalist give the Western finalists an equal chance at the Cup. Montréal acquiesced and still won every game to take home its second Stanley Cup in franchise history and its first in the NHL. The Morenz, Joliat and Boucher line scored 12 of the 14 playoff goals.

Toronto

Before opening up a new season and a new building, Conn Smythe knew he needed to add one more ingredient to his team that would make it a true Stanley Cup contender. Smythe was not happy with Leafs coach Art Duncan after the team bowed out of the playoffs against the Chicago Black Hawks in the 1931 quarterfinals. Smythe wanted a character like himself behind the bench, someone who would speak his mind and not shy away from dismantling a player if he wasn't playing up to team standards. Smythe found all these qualities in Dick Irvin.

As a player, Dick Irvin was known for his work ethic and for his ability to put the puck in the net. But when a fractured skull forced him to hang up his skates, Irvin could not tear himself away from the game and was offered the position of head coach for his old team, the Chicago Black Hawks. In his first full year with the Hawks, Coach Irvin took his team all the way to the Stanley Cup finals, only to lose to the Montréal Canadiens in the final game.

When Smythe learned that Irvin had been cut loose by the Chicago Black Hawks before the start of the 1931-32 season, he knew he could get the coach he wanted for his Leafs. A few games into that season, Smythe had had enough with Art Duncan. Smythe phoned Irvin in Chicago and asked him to coach in Toronto; Irvin accepted and took his place behind the bench on November 28, 1931.

To make his transition to the team a little easier and to give Irvin more time to get to know his players, Smythe took the coaching reins for the first game while Irvin sat on the sidelines and observed. The idea was to ease Irvin slowly into his coaching job, but when the Boston Bruins came back to tie the game 4-4, Smythe turned to Irvin and handed him the job. The game ended up going into overtime, with the Leafs winning 6-5.

Once at the helm, he set about making a few changes that would make his good players become great. Irvin knew he had a good team to work with, but that they lacked the work ethic and discipline that could make them Stanley Cup champions. Irvin put his team through strenuous workouts and constant practices, stressing that the players stick to a disciplined, systematic game. Irvin knew that if they played as a team and stuck to the system, they could be the best in the NHL. Everything appeared to be going according to Irvin's plan as the Leafs took over first place in the Canadian Division by December 22 after a 9-3 victory over the New York Americans.

Although the "Kid Line" of Charlie Conacher, Joe Primeau and Busher Jackson was responsible for the majority of the scoring, Irvin was getting a well-rounded effort from the rest of the team. Hap Day, Harold Darragh and King Clancy provided the Leafs with the defensive system they needed, making them tough to beat every time they hit the ice.

Conn Smythe continued to smile as the season progressed, and his team drew large crowds to the Maple Leaf Gardens, grossing tickets revenues that had never been seen at the old Mutual Street Arena. As the season continued and the Leafs remained in a head-to-head battle with the Montréal Canadiens for first place in the Canadian Division, interest in the Toronto team just kept growing. This was a surprise to many during a time when other teams around the league were struggling because of the Depression. The Leafs regularly had a full house and on the days when the Montréal Canadiens came to town, the Gardens arena was completely sold out.

In one game on February 13, 1932, the Maple Leafs trounced the Canadiens in a 6-0 victory that saw nine major penalties after a free-for-all fight. Several players were fined $25 by NHL president Frank Calder for their involvement in the fracas. The rough play as teams fought for a spot in the playoffs continued into the last few games of the season. Even Conn Smythe got involved in some on-ice action.

On March 15, 1932, the Leafs were in Boston with just four games remaining in the regular season and were in a heated race with the Canadiens for first place in the Canadian division. Every win counted, and the Leafs general manager placed himself behind the bench for the remaining games to ensure his team was playing its best. But the Leafs were not doing well against the Bruins that night, and Smythe quickly lost his temper when, with the score tied, Toronto goaltender Lorne Chabot tripped Boston's Cooney Weiland as he passed by Chabot's net. Referee Bill Stewart spotted the infraction and gave Chabot a two-minute penalty. While Chabot was in the box, the Bruins managed to put in three goals past the defencemen left in charge of guarding the net (at that time, goaltenders had to serve their own penalties). After the third goal was scored, Conn Smythe's face turned bright red. Fuming over the injustice done to his team, Smythe grabbed the referee by the sweater as he skated by the Toronto bench and berated him for Chabot's penalty. The referee then ordered Smythe to leave his spot behind the bench, and when Smythe refused, arena attendants were called to physically remove him. Seeing their manager being forcefully removed, several players joined in the melee and threw some punches. More players and attendants joined the fight, and Boston Bruins president Charles Adams had to bring in the police to restore order. Conn Smythe had the last word in the end, retaking his spot behind the Leafs bench for the rest of the game as coach. The Leafs lost by a final score of 6-2.

Toronto finished the season just behind the Montréal Canadiens in their division and third overall in the league, only one point behind the Rangers. Busher Jackson and Joe Primeau finished at the top of the scoring race while their line mate Charlie Conacher was tied with the Rangers' Bill Cook as leading goal scorers.

Toronto started its playoff run in Chicago on March 27, 1932, taking on the Black Hawks in a rematch of the previous year's quarterfinals. Having coached in Chicago, Dick Irvin knew very well what his team had to do to defeat the Hawks. Irvin knew that if his scoring lines could break Chicago's defensive wall and get a few pucks past Vezina Trophy-winning goaltender Charlie Gardiner, then the Leafs could easily run away with the series. The Hawks were not much of a threat on offence, having scored only 86 goals during the regular season compared to the Leafs' 155. The defensive duo of Clarence "Taffy" Abel and Marvin "Cyclone" Wentworth had been keeping forwards out of their zone all season long and didn't changed their tactics for the first game against Toronto.

The Leafs' sharpshooters were continually frustrated by Chicago's tight defensive style, and when they did manage a shot on net, they could put nothing by the superb Gardiner. Lorne Chabot was doing his part to keep his team in the game by making some brilliant saves, but the Leafs were simply out-worked, and it was only a matter of time before the Hawks put one in. Gerry Lowrey, who managed to score only 8 goals during the regular season, scored the winning goal in the third period, ending the game with a less-than-exciting 1-0 victory.

The second and final game of the total-goal series was a completely different affair. Chicago waltzed into Maple Leaf Gardens confident that their defensive system could handle anything the speedy Leafs forwards could throw at them, and that if Toronto got around their defence, they could always rely on Gardiner to keep them in the game.

The Gardens was filled to capacity with eager fans hoping for some sweet retribution for the team that eliminated them in last year's playoffs. Irvin made a few minor adjustments to compensate for the defensive system of the Hawks and found that his players responded very well. The fans who packed the Gardens stood for almost the entire game as they watched their Leafs trounce the Hawks in a 6-1 rout. Charlie Conacher was the star of the game with two goals. The fans in the Gardens roared with approval as the Leafs exacted their revenge on the Hawks and earned a spot in the next round against the Montréal Maroons.

The Maple Leafs were the favourites in the semi-finals against the Maroons, but with veteran talent including Nels Stewart and Lionel Conacher (Charlie's brother) the Leafs knew they could not take them for granted. It was a tough defensive game held in Montréal with neither team dominating. Charlie Conacher got the first goal after stick-handling his way past brother Lionel and putting a fancy move on goaltender Flat Walsh. The Maroons equalled the score late in the third period when Dave Trottier put in the tying goal.

The second game was held in Toronto before a record crowd of 14,000 eager fans. Irvin drilled his players before the game, hoping to make them understand that if they stuck to the system that got them past the Black Hawks, they would have no problem making it past the Maroons.

The Leafs looked a little nervous as they made their way through the first moments of the first period. Even a goal by the Leafs' Red Horner could not shake off their nerves as the Maroons came back with two goals of their own by Jimmy Ward and Babe Siebert and carried that lead well into the third period. Every time the Leafs got the puck, the Maroons were at their heels trying to take it away from them or dump it back into the Leafs zone. With little time remaining in the game, the fans at the Gardens got to their feet and lifted the roof with a roar. The Leafs were all standing on the bench, screaming words of support at their teammates on the ice, intensifying the tense atmosphere in the Gardens.

A hush fell as Hap Day broke away with the puck on an individual rush toward Maroons goaltender Flat Walsh. The fans held their breath as Day made his move on Walsh from in close and put the puck in the net to tie the game. The Gardens exploded, cheering for Toronto's captain for three straight minutes. Neither team could put in another goal to break the tie before the third period ended, sending the game into sudden-death overtime.

Both teams were a little apprehensive in the first few minutes of overtime, not wanting to open up any opportunities for the other. Irvin kept up the pressure on his players to push forward and take the risks needed to win the series and make it to the Stanley Cup finals. He knew that if the Maroons broke into the Leafs zone, he had one of the best goaltenders in Lorne Chabot to stop whatever the Maroons could produce. At the 18th minute of the first overtime period the Leafs' Bob Gracie finally broke the deadlock, putting a shot past Flat Walsh for the victory. The Gardens erupted as the Leafs cleared their bench and swarmed Gracie. Toronto was on to the next stage to face the New York Rangers for the Cup.

Although the Rangers finished the regular season with more points and had a week off before the start of the Stanley Cup finals against the Leafs, they looked shaky in the opening game of the series. Former Leafs goaltender John Ross Roach looked unsteady before the hometown crowd of about 16,000 screaming Rangers fans. Both goaltenders' jobs were made all the more difficult as the game was rife with penalties—some 20 had been dealt out to both teams by the end of the game. But when all the smoke cleared, the Leafs were victorious with a 6-4 victory. Busher Jackson was the star for Toronto, scoring a hat trick.

In what can be viewed as a sign of how much hockey mattered to American audiences in the early days, game two of the Stanley Cup finals had to be moved out of Madison Square Garden to Boston Garden because of a scheduling conflict with a circus. Despite the fact that the Bruins weren't playing in the final, 12,000 die-hard Boston hockey fans still showed up to see the Rangers and the Leafs play. The Rangers quickly secured themselves a two-goal lead but completely fell apart later in the game when King Clancy and Charlie Conacher potted two goals each. John Ross Roach was just not playing the way he had against the Montréal Canadiens in the Rangers' first series, and let in another six goals. The game ended with the Leafs scoring six and the Rangers only two. The Rangers were now on the verge of losing their chance at winning the Cup in the best-of-five series.

Back in Toronto in front of their hometown fans, the Leafs were confident they could end the series with a strong performance.

Before a capacity crowd of 14,366 at the Maple Leaf Gardens, the Leafs played a great game of hockey. They controlled most of the game despite the hat trick by Rangers forward Frank Boucher. John Ross Roach was again the difference in the game, looking like a nervous rookie in the Rangers net and letting in a number of easy shots. When the final buzzer sounded, Toronto had won the game and their first Stanley Cup as the Maple Leafs. The "Gashouse Gang," as the Leafs had come to be known, had electrified the city with their Cup win and would continue to dominate the National Hockey League as the decade went on.

Boston

The 1928-29 Boston Bruins had an imposing line-up of skilled players. Goaltender Cecil Thompson was one of the top goaltenders in the league that season, Eddie Shore and Lionel Hitchman presented opponents a formidable wall on defence, and Ralph Weiland, Dit Clapper and Dutch Gainor were known as the "dynamite line." With that all-star line-up, the Bruins finished in second place overall behind the Canadiens.

They would face the Canadiens in the opening round of the playoffs and sweep the best-of-five series. The Canadiens were a strong team, and going into the playoffs, they had their goaltender at the peak of his career. George Hainsworth recorded 22 shutouts and a goals against average of 0.92 during the regular season. But it was the offensive skills of the Bruins forwards and the defensive wall that kept the Canadiens at bay. The win against the Canadiens propelled the Bruins directly into the finals against the New York Rangers.

It was the first time in Stanley Cup history that two American teams played for the championship. Boston was able to capture the first game of the best-of-three series with a 2-0 win. Two nights later Bill Carson of the Bruins scored with less than two minutes left in the game to give Boston the 2-1 victory and the Stanley Cup win. A wild celebration greeted the Bruins players upon their return from New York. Any time a Boston team beats New York, no matter the sport, there is always a big celebration. Manager Art Ross summed up the spirit of his team that year: "There has never been a professional team where there has been less bickering, fewer jealousies and better spirit. All season long, that has been the case."

Detroit

The Detroit Red Wings had the legendary Jack Adams behind the bench when they won their first Stanley Cup. The fiery coach was both loved and hated by his players, but they all respected him. He had led them through a tough season in 1935-36 in which most players were forced out of playing at one time or another due to injury, but still Adams managed to coach his way through the difficulties and lead his team to end first place overall. With the regular season out of the way, the Wings moved into the opening round of the playoffs against the skilled Montréal Maroons. The first game of the series turned out to be a memorable one.

On March 24, 1936, Detroit's Normie Smith and the Maroons' Lorne Chabot were the opposing goaltenders as they faced off before a sold-out crowd at the Montréal Forum for game one of the series. After three periods of play, the score was still tied at zero as both goaltenders were unwilling to give up any ground in the game. The deadlock would continue through the first OT period, then a second, a third, then a fourth and fifth finally before the Red Wings Mud Bruneteau scored the winner at 2:25 AM, at 16:30 of the sixth overtime period! Normie Smith recorded a shutout in the longest game in NHL history ever played—a total of 176 minutes and 30 seconds.

After the loss, the Maroons seemed spent of energy, and the Red Wings finished the best-of-five series in three straight. Leaping directly into the Stanley Cup finals, the Red Wings faced off against the Toronto Maple Leafs. It would be anyone's series. The regular season saw the Leafs finish just four points behind the Wings, and they had the legendary Georges Hainsworth in nets.

However, the Maple Leafs were no match for the Wings, and the Wings skated off with the team's first Stanley Cup. The next year the Red Wings won their second Stanley Cup.

Ottawa

In the first decade of professional hockey, the Ottawa Senators were by far the league's best with legendary players such as Frank Nighbor, Jack Darragh, Clint Benedict, Punch Broadbent and Corb Denneny.

By the end of the 1919-20 regular season, the Senators had won both halves thereby negating the need for an NHL final. (Up until the 1921-22, the NHL split its regular season schedule into two halves, with the winner of each half meeting in the NHL finals for the right to play for the Stanley Cup.) The Sens moved straight to the Stanley Cup finals versus the PCHA champion Seattle Metropolitans. Seattle made the long journey across the country to play the first game on March 22, 1920, at Ottawa's Dey's Arena.

Since the arena had natural ice, the Stanley Cup finals were at the mercy of the weather, and unfortunately for that week, the Ottawa region was having an unseasonably warm spring. With the temperature hovering around the freezing mark, the condition of the ice was of prime concern for both sides. When both teams hit the ice for the first face-off, they noticed right away that it wasn't going to be an easy game. Within a few minutes, the 12 players had chipped enough holes and ruts in the ice to make it tough going for the remaining periods. The two teams battled each other and the ice for three tough periods, with the Senators coming out the victors by a score of 3-2. Before another sell-out crowd of 7500, the Ottawa Senators played the second game at Dey's Arena on a rink covered with a thin layer of water. The warming trend in the weather combined with the heat generated by 7500 excited fans made for a difficult game for both teams. The one player who didn't mind the conditions was Senators goaltender Clint Benedict, who saw very little work during the game and ended up with a 3-0 shutout victory. Unfortunately, the play on the ice was not the story of game three, since once again the condition of the ice took centre stage. Players were forced to play the game on a surface covered by more than one inch of water. This made for an interesting and very wet game. Seattle won by a score of 3-1. The goaltenders could hardly be blamed for letting in the goals because behind every shot on net came a blast of cold water in their faces. With the weather forecast calling for increasing temperatures in Ottawa, it was decided to move the series to the artificial ice surface of the Mutual Street Arena in Toronto. On the better ice surface, the pace of the game picked up and so did the scoring as the Metropolitans won the fourth game 5-2, forcing the fifth and deciding game of the best-of-five series.

Clint Benedict played one of his best games of the series, stopping all but one of Seattle's shots on goal. Benedict's teammates did the rest of the work, popping in six goals past Metropolitans goaltender Harry "Hap" Holmes. When the final buzzer sounded, the Ottawa Senators had won the game by a final score of 6-1, won the series three games to two and celebrated their sixth Stanley Cup championship in franchise history and their first Cup in the NHL.

New Jersey
The 1994-95 season will forever be a statistical anomaly. Because of the National Hockey League

players strike, hockey fans did not get to see their first games until the season began on January 20, 1994. The season was cut down to 48 games (the first time since the 1941-42 season, but the playoffs would retain the same format as previous years.

The New Jersey Devils started life out in the NHL as the Kansas City Scouts in 1974, then as the Colorado Rockies, before finally settling in East Rutherford, New Jersey, in 1982. The franchise had consistently underachieved until the early 1990s when the franchise fortunes began to turn around.

The Devils had some decent goaltenders in their brief history in the league, but no one as talented or determined as Martin Brodeur who made his debut with the team during the 1993-94 season. In 47 games played Brodeur only lost 11. He was a major reason that for the first time the Devils finished in the top five in the league and entered into the playoffs looking like serious contenders.

They did win the first two rounds in the '94 playoffs, but the wins did not come easily. Jersey had to get by a difficult Buffalo Sabres and their skilled netminder Dominik Hasek. It took seven games, but Brodeur out-played and out-lasted his rival. The Devils then took six hard fought games before they put the Bruins on the golf course for the summer. The New York Rangers were a different matter.

All hope for the New York Rangers seemed to be fading after the Devils won game five and moved to a 3-2 series lead. It didn't look good for the Rangers and that ugly curse on the blueshirts that had kept the Cup off of Broadway for 54 years appeared to be rearing its ugly head again. But an inspirational speech by Rangers captain, veteran Mark Messier, provided the motivation needed for the Rangers to shock the Devils in an overtime game seven victory. The Rangers went on to win the Cup and sent the Devils packing.

With the chance of winning the Cup so brutally taken away, the Devils returned to the shortened season with renewed hopes. They had a future Hall of Fame candidate between the pipes and the brains of head coach Jacques Lemaire behind the bench. Since joining the team in 1993-94, Lemaire had instituted a new playing style to the Devils line-up that would change the league forever.

Never having that pure goal-scoring forward so desired by teams, the Devils were never that much of an offensive threat. They had skilled players but none had ever been able to lead the team to putting points on the board. Because of this,

Lemaire developed a defensive system that was dubbed "the trap." This style involved an overwhelming emphasis on defence. When the opposing team tried to cross on a neutral zone rush, Lemaire would tell his players to block the lanes and stop any forward momentum into the zone. The system proved effective, and the Devils won games. This, however, made for tedious games with little offence. The added fact of having one of the best young goaltenders in the league propelled Jersey through Boston, Pittsburgh and Philadelphia in the 1995 playoff run. Jersey was so effective at it they shut down the Detroit Red Wings in the Stanley Cup finals in four straight games to win the franchise's first Cup. The Devils also won the Cup in 2000 and again 2003.

Tampa Bay

Since joining the league for the 1992-93 season, the Tampa Bay Lightning suffered season after season of mediocre hockey that saw them miss the playoffs nine out of their first 10 times. The direction of the franchise shifted with the addition of a certain group of players that were all peaking in their careers at the right moment. Vincent Lecavalier, Martin St. Louis, Brad Richards and goaltender Nikolai Khabibulin all joined the team around the 2000-01 season, and fans of the franchise finally got to see quality hockey on the ice.

Lecavalier began to establish himself as one of the best forwards in the league, and his linemate Martin St. Louis surprised the league by becoming one of the top point getters. The Lightning went from the bottom of the league straight to one of the best by the end of the 2002-03 season. Although they were eliminated from the playoffs (by the eventual Stanley Cup–winning New Jersey Devils), the group of young players had learned the valuable lessons that only come with losing. They returned for the 2003-04 season with renewed hopes.

Finishing the season second best overall in the league, with the league's leading scorer Martin St. Louis and with Khabibulin having a career season, the Lightning entered the 2004 playoffs as one of the top contenders for the Cup.

In the first round, the Lightning were barely tested against the Alexei Yashin–led New York Islanders, beating them in five games and with goaltender Khabibulin racking up three playoff shutouts in the process. Next, the Montréal Canadiens fell to the side in a four game sweep. The true test of the team's strength came in the conference finals against the Philadelphia Flyers. Both squads traded victories, taking the series to game seven before Tampa's Frederick Modin notched the game winner sending the franchise into the Stanley Cup finals for the first time in their short history against a tough Calgary Flames team.

The Flames had battled for each and every victory in their run to the finals. Flames fever seemed to grip hockey fans everywhere and many had the Lightning set to get burned in the series. The Lightning might not have had the Cinderella story playoff run that followed the Flames, but they played good solid hockey and it proved effective. The Flames were fuelled with passion and hard-working players that Stanley Cup–winning teams always have. It promised to be an entertaining series.

After trading wins, Calgary won the decisive game five that put them ahead in the series 3-2. This wasn't a position the Lightning had to deal with all playoffs, and they knew Calgary would fight to take the series in six. Game six in Calgary was a loud affair. Calgary fans turned the arena red wearing their team's colours and turned up the volume so loud that the roof nearly came off. But Tampa would not be denied easily. Brad Richards scored a pair of goals for the Lightning sending the game into overtime. All Calgary needed was one goal to win the Stanley

Cup before the hometown crowd, but it was Martin St. Louis who got the game winner in double overtime. The series would have to be decided in the seventh game.

Back in Tampa before their hometown crowd, the Lightning got two goals by Ruslan Fedotenko in both the first and second periods while goaltender Khabibulin only let one slip by. The Flames tried hard to slip one past him to tie the game with 16 shots in the dying moments, but the goaltender came up with the performance of his career. It was a brilliant run by the Lightning in the playoffs. After two easy opening round series, they proved themselves to be a hockey club that could fight it out and grind with the best teams in the league.

Philadelphia

During the 1972-73 season, the Philadelphia Flyers finished with their first winning record since joining the league in 1967. Leading the way for the Flyers that season was a young Bobby Clarke, whose skill in front of the net earned him second place in the NHL scoring race behind Phil Esposito with 104 points. Rounding out the Flyers offence were big forwards like Rick MacLeish, Reggie Leach and Bill Barber—all three players 50 goal scorers during their time in a Philadelphia uniform. They earned the nickname the "Broad Street Bullies" from their aggressive style of play with names like Dave "the Hammer" Schultz, Don Saleski and Andre "Moose" Dupont. They might not have won all their games in the most convincing of fashions, but the team always managed to get things done with a combination of offensive talent, excellent goaltending, sheer terror and the desire to win. A style dreamt up by the Flyers astute coach Freddy "The Fog" Shero who knew that psychology was a big factor in hockey. If another team knew you were going to hit them every time you touched a puck, then the next time you had it on the end of your stick you would think twice before deciding what to do with it, and that's all the Flyers required for motivation. Shero made sure his players knew his philosophy. "Get to the puck by the shortest route and arrive there in ill-humour," read the sign posted in the Philadelphia dressing room.

The Flyers also had another weapon up their sleeves, and her name was Kate Smith. No, she didn't lace on a pair of skates, but it seemed that every time she sang "God Bless America" at Flyers home games, they tended to win. Her record for the Flyers in the seven years when they occasionally substituted the national anthem for her "God Bless America" was an incredible 36-3-1. Whether it was the words to the song or the tone of her voice, something about Kate Smith's version of "God Bless America" inspired the Flyers, and they carried these winning ways into the 1974 Stanley Cup Playoffs.

After finishing the season strong, the Flyers entered into the playoffs as the division favourites. They dispensed of their opening round opponents to make it into the Stanley Cup final for the first time in the team's short history.

Colorado

In the final year of existence of the Québec Nordiques, it was felt that the team was on the verge of making a charge at the Stanley Cup for the first time in its history. But that is exactly when economics got in the way and forced the Nordiques to pack up the franchise and move to Colorado for the start of the 1995-96 season.

In Colorado, as the Avalanche, the team prospered but they became a real contender when Patrick Roy joined the team halfway through the season from Montréal. It was a huge loss for Montréal but a huge gain for Colorado.

Roy helped the Avalanche finish the season at the top of their division and as one of the favourites to make it into the finals. In the opening round of the playoffs against the Vancouver Canucks, Colorado dispensed with their challengers in six games. In the conference semi-finals they faced a tough challenge against the Chicago Black Hawks, but they again prevailed in six games.

The conference final against the Detroit Red Wings was the true test for the Avalanche. Detroit's Wings were the regular season champions, and they had built up a healthy rivalry throughout the season. But it would be the Avalanche who prevailed again in six games. Patrick Roy was playing at the top of his game, and the Red Wings snipers could not get the pucks into the net.

In the finals, the Avalanche faced off against the Florida Panthers. But the Panthers could not match the skill of Colorado, and the series was finished in four straight games. Colorado had its first Stanley Cup.

Calgary

Toward the end of the 1980s, the Calgary Flames were caught under the shadow of their provincial rivals, the Edmonton Oilers. They had knocked them off in 1986 after the Oilers' Steve Smith had graciously eliminated his own team by scoring the series-winning goal on his own net. But having passed the Oilers, the Flames faced off against a young Montréal Canadiens team led by rookie goaltending sensation Patrick Roy. The Flames managed to take the first game, but the Canadiens rebounded and won the series and the Stanley Cup in five games.

It was a tough pill for some of the Flames players to swallow, but the loss was a valuable lesson for the team, one that would carry them straight to the top of the league just three years later.

The Flames were having an excellent season, but they still needed more grit on the team if they were going to make it far into the playoffs. To that end, they reached down into their farm team, now in Salt Lake City, Utah, and called up Theoren Fleury, who was having an outstanding season at the minor pro level. They needed his gritty approach to the game. In December 1987, Fleury had been selected by Team Canada to represent the country at the annual World Junior Hockey Championship. Fleury ended up squaring off in a fight with a Soviet player, and it quickly snowballed into a bench-clearing brawl, resulting in the suspension of both teams from the tournament. The Flames wanted grit, and Fleury had plenty to give. With the Flames, he scored almost a point per game and finished the year with 14 goals and 20 assists.

In the playoffs, the Flames were a team determined to make into the finals after a tough seven-game series against the Vancouver Canucks that needed overtime to solve. The decisive goal occurred when the Flames Jim Peplinski crossed the Vancouver blue line in transition and did what any good hockey player without a scoring chance would do—he just threw the puck on net and prayed something would happen. Something did. The puck bounced off Calgary's Joel Otto's skate as he was tangling with a Vancouver defenceman in front of goaltender Kirk Maclean. The puck slipped by unnoticed into the back of the net. The Calgary fans erupted in jubilation and relief as the Flames took the first round by a score of 4-3.

Calgary then handed the LA Kings a swift defeat in four straight games in the division finals and then another quick five-game upset over the Chicago Black Hawks. It was time for the Stanley Cup finals against 1986 opponents the Montréal Canadiens.

Calgary established their dominance in the first game of the finals with a 3-2 victory at home. Montréal won the next game, and both teams flew back to Montréal for games three and four. Again, both teams won a game and flew back to Calgary to play the important game five. It was a close battle, but Calgary goaltender Mike Vernon made all the stops necessary to give his team a 3-2 victory and the series lead going back to Montréal.

The atmosphere in the Forum that night was tense. No team had ever beaten the Montréal Canadiens in the Montréal Forum in the playoffs before and the hometown fans did not want to witness a historical first.

Flames forward Colin Patterson scored the only goal of the first period, but the Canadiens' Claude Lemieux erased the Flames lead early in the second period. Lanny McDonald then put the Flames back ahead 2-1. Then Calgary's Doug Gilmour potted the insurance goal to put the Flames in strong command of the game. The Canadiens tried to even the score by pulling goaltender Patrick Roy, but the series and the Stanley Cup were put completely out of reach when Gilmour slipped in the empty-net goal for the victory and the Stanley Cup. After 17 years as a franchise—first as the Atlanta Flames and nine in Calgary—the Flames had finally won a Stanley Cup.

Edmonton
The first four years of Edmonton Oilers franchise can be summed up rather easily. Wayne Gretzky. The young phenom had been tearing up the league since joining the NHL, and sports fans watched with baited breath just how long it would take him to lead the team to the Stanley Cup. After all, any player who can score 92 goals in one season is a team leader, and great things

are expected. In just the team's fourth year of existence, the Oilers made it all the way to the Stanley Cup final in 1983 only to be denied the Cup by reigning champs—the New York Islanders. The Oilers were a young team, and most pundits said that it was only a matter of time given the depth of talent on the team that they would again knock on Stanley's door.

In 1983-84 season, the Oilers finished first in the league and had achieved the prolific scoring record of putting in 446 goals during the season. The Oilers were a fast, high-scoring team, and opponents could do little to contain the beast.

In the playoffs, the Oilers played the Winnipeg Jets in the opening round, defeating them easily in three straight games of a best-of-five series. Calgary provided the toughest challenge to the young squad, forcing a deciding game seven before the Oilers moved on to an easy conference final four-game sweep of the Minnesota North Stars. For the second year in a row, the Oilers made it into the Stanley Cup finals against the New York Islanders.

In the first game in New York, it was apparent that both teams were not playing at full speed, choosing rather to play it safe than lose momentum in the first match. The Oilers scored high in the regular season but came out with an uncharacteristic 1-0 victory. The aging Islanders squad managed to pull out a 6-1 victory in game two, but the Oilers took control of the series in the third game and never looked back. The Oilers won the next three straight games finishing off the Islanders 5-2 before a home crowd. Wayne Gretzky beamed like a 10-year-old kid as NHL president John Ziegler handed him the Cup for the first time. The Oilers repeated as champs the next year, again in 1987, 1988 and in 1990.

New York Rangers

The story of the 1928 Stanley Cup finals between the New York Rangers and the Montréal Maroons is almost mythical.

The 1927-28 New York Rangers, coached by the coaching of hockey legend Lester Patrick, had a powerful scoring line-up with players such as Bun Cook, Frank Boucher and Bill Cook. When added to the solid defensive core of Ivan "Ching" Johnson and the goaltending of Lorne Chabot, the Rangers had a team that could match the equally adept Maroons at every level as long as everyone stayed healthy and as any coach will tell you, the playoff season has a way of injuring key players at the worst moments.

Having to play the entire series in Montréal because of a scheduling conflict at Madison

Square Garden with the circus, the Rangers did not get off to a great start. Before a jubilant hometown crowd, the Maroons potted goals in the second and third periods of the first game, while their netminder, Clint Benedict, stopped every shot that came his way for the 2-0 victory. Going into the second game, Patrick knew his team would have to get men in front of Benedict because, if he saw the puck coming, there was no way he would miss the save.

In the second game, the Maroons had excellent scoring power, but it was the goaltending of Clint Benedict that the Rangers needed to solve in order to win. With the usual fanfare of a game played at the Montréal Forum, play got underway, and Patrick put his best defensive line-up against the Maroons scoring line led by Nels Stewart. All was going according to plan in the first few minutes of the game when fate intervened and made this series and this game in particular one to remember.

At just the four-minute mark of the first period, Maroons star Nels Stewart broke into the Rangers zone and let loose a bullet of a shot that struck Rangers goaltender Lorne Chabot in the eye. Chabot hit the ice unconscious and bleeding profusely. As paramedics strapped Chabot onto a stretcher, Patrick was left to deal with the fact that he had no other goaltender to replace Chabot for the rest of the game.

To everyone's astonishment, Patrick suited up in Chabot's gear and took to the ice. The 44-year-old Rangers head coach was no stranger to the game of hockey, but the last time he played, he didn't have any grey hair.

Eddie Girard was left open-mouthed as Patrick played a brilliant game in front of his boys only allowing one goal in a 2-1 overtime victory. Chabot returned from his injury and helped the Rangers defeat the Maroons in the best-of-five series to win the franchise's first Stanley Cup. In all, the Rangers have won three Cups.

NY Islanders

Most expansion teams, when they first enter the NHL, spend their first few seasons at the bottom of their division, working out the kinks in their system before they can truly challenge the more established teams. Although they gradually improved throughout the 1970s, the Islanders still hadn't blossomed into the dynasty of the '80s. The addition of key players such as Mike Bossy, Bryan Trottier and Clark Gilles assured the New York Isles' faithful of a successful future. The team came close to taking the Cup in the late 1970s, but they had to compete against the Philadelphia

Flyers and the Montréal Canadiens at their peak. However, the Isles wouldn't have to wait long for their turn.

The Islanders got their chance in the 1980 playoffs. They had finished with a respectable 91 points during the regular season but were not favoured in the race for Lord Stanley's Cup. The Philadelphia Flyers and the defending champions, the Montréal Canadiens, were at top of the league and had some of the better veteran players. But as everyone who knows something about hockey will say, the playoffs are a whole new season, and the 1980 playoffs would be all about the New York Islanders.

In the preliminary rounds, the Isles easily took out the Los Angeles Kings, and in an overtime-laden quarterfinals, they squeaked by the Boston Bruins in five games and the Buffalo Sabres in a high-scoring six-game series to make it to the Stanley Cup finals for the first time in franchise history. It wasn't going to be an easy win for the Islanders, since they were facing the Philadelphia powerhouse that finished the regular season on top of the NHL with 116 points.

The final series turned out to be one of the most exciting in recent memory after the long four years of domination by the Montréal Canadiens and their strong defensive core. The first game in

Philadelphia was a close one, however, with the Islanders coming out on top 4-3 in overtime. But game two saw everything open up, and the Flyers delivered a clear message with an 8-3 pounding. The Islanders regrouped and returned the favour with two straight wins with all lines contributing to 6-2 and 5-2 victories to take a 3-1 series lead. Philly took game five easily by a score of 6-3 before a nervous hometown crowd to stay alive and send the series into game six.

Philadelphia coach Pat Quinn decided to tighten up on defence for game six in order to hold back the powerful offensive unit of the Islanders. He was hoping to get ahead early in the game and use a tight defensive style to hold the lead. At first, everything seemed to be working in the Flyers' favour, but the Islanders had the same plan in mind, and when the final buzzer sounded the end of regulation time, the score was deadlocked at 3-3. In the first few minutes of overtime, both teams were a little skittish about trying any daring offensive moves, but as it looked like the game might go on longer than they wanted, the forwards took some chances on rushes with the defencemen joining in right behind. Both had chances, but neither Isles goalie Billy Smith nor Philly goalie Pete Peeters wanted to be the one to let in a goal. It was at the lucky 7:11 mark of the period that the game finally ended.

The Islanders flew into the Flyers zone with the puck and got it back to the point. Flyers goaltender Pete Peeters searched frantically for the puck through a mess of bodies in front of his net, but pesky Isles forward Bob Nystrom wasn't going to move from his prime piece of real estate. After taking some abuse in front of the net, the shot finally came in, and Nystrom got just enough of a deflection on his backhand to put it over Peeters and into the net for the Stanley Cup–winning goal.

"I really didn't think it was going to go in," said Nystrom after the game. "I never scored a goal on my backhand all year. I had to get it high, and sure enough, it went high."

"Until that moment, we were considered a team of losers and chokers," said Islanders coach Al Arbour with a huge smile across his face after the game. "If Nystrom doesn't score, who knows what happens to our team?"

The Islanders were just the second new team to win the Stanley Cup since the league had expanded in 1967, and they would continue the tradition into the next season at the expense of the surprise finalists, the Minnesota North Stars. The Islanders were even better the next season, using the same mix of offence and defence that made the Montréal Canadiens so successful in the late 1970s. The Pittsburgh Penguins were the only team to challenge them in the 1982 playoffs, losing to the Isles in overtime of the final game of the division semi-finals. After that, it was smooth sailing for the Islanders, as they took care of the New York Rangers, Québec Nordiques and Vancouver Canucks for their third straight Stanley Cup. They did it again the next year, making it all the way to the finals, this time against the Edmonton Oilers and their young team of future Hall of Famers. The Oilers lost to the Islanders, but they learned their lesson for the 1984 playoff finals, when both teams met again. But that time it was the Oilers who came out on top and started a dynasty of their own.

Victoria Cougars

Based in the Western Canadian Hockey League, the Victoria Cougars won the Stanley Cup in 1925, becoming the last non-NHL team to do so. Led by famed hockey man Lester Patrick, the Cougars earned the right to play for the Stanley Cup by winning their division championship, beating out league rivals Saskatoon and Calgary for that honour.

The Cougars had a solid line-up of long-time hockey players, Frank Foyston and Frank Fredrickson, and most notably goaltender Harry "Hap" Holmes. But it was the cunning hockey mind of Lester Patrick that brought the team together and made them a threat on the ice. The Cougars would have the initial advantage in the Stanley Cup finals of playing the entire series at home in Victoria but their opponents, the Montréal Canadiens, were the reigning Stanley Cup champs, and they had the killer scoring duo of Howie Morenz and Aurel Joliat to back them up. It was going to be a tough series that could swing either way.

The Cougars won the first game 5-2 against a visibly tired Canadiens squad. The Habs had arrived a few days before the series and did not seem to have their legs under them to match the skating of the Cougars. The Canadiens lost game two by a closer score of 3-1, but they just could not find the power behind their game. The Cougars won the best-of-five series in four games to become the last non-NHL team to win the Stanley Cup.

Chicago

After a horrible season just one year earlier, the Chicago Black Hawks began the 1933-34 NHL season with little hope of making any significant improvements. The Hawks had little to no scoring depth on their team, but they had a solid defence, and most importantly, they had Charlie Gardiner in nets.

Gardiner was the only reason the Hawks remained a competitive team. He carried the team on his performance to the Stanley Cup finals in 1931 (where they lost to the Montréal Canadiens) and had remained one of the top goaltenders in the league through the early '30s. By the time the 1933-34 season began Gardiner had nearly resigned himself to never having the chance at winning the Cup. Throughout the season, it seemed the Hawks were resigned to that fact as well. They only managed to score 88 goals in 48 games. When compared to the Toronto Maple Leafs' 174 goals, the Hawks did not seem to have a chance of making it far in the post season. However, while they did only score 88 goals, with the help of Charlie Gardiner, the Hawks had the lowest GAA in the league with 83. The Hawks never outscored an opponent by much, but they still managed to win a few games.

Going into the playoffs, Charlie Gardiner was playing the best hockey of his career. His backstopping brilliance enabled the Hawks to come out with series wins against the Montréal Canadiens and the Montréal Maroons to get them into the Stanley Cup finals against the Detroit Red Wings.

Not one hockey pundit at the time gave the Hawks much of a chance against the more skilled Red Wings and with good reason. In the previous four years, the Hawks had not won a single regular season or playoff game against the Wings. It was going to be a test for the Hawks, but they felt their chances were good with Gardiner in goal. They were right.

Gardiner nearly stood on his head to make saves in the first game of the series that needed double overtime before the Hawks put the game away. Two nights later Gardiner was just as impressive in a 4-1 victory over the Wings. Detroit managed to break Gardiner's composure in game three putting an uncharacteristic five goals in his net in a 5-2 Hawks loss. The fourth game ended in regulation time with no goals scored on either side. The Wings, facing elimination, were holding back in their zone not wanting to give up a soft goal. It proved to be a bad strategy. Gardiner kept his team alive until Chicago's Mush March scored the winner in the second overtime to give the city of Chicago its first Stanley Cup. Gardiner's effort in the final game remains the only double overtime shutout in the history of the Stanley Cup finals.

Carolina
With the smallest market-base in the league at the time, the Hartford Whalers were having trouble remaining financially viable in the new NHL. By the 1996-97 season, owners looked to another city to save its franchise. That city was

Raleigh, North Carolina. After all, since 1979, when the Hartford Whalers had entered the league, the franchise had not won a Stanley Cup and had only one playoff series in their history. It was time for a new outlook, and so the Carolina Hurricanes were born.

At the beginning of the 1997-98 inaugural season, no one gave the team much hope of success in a U.S. market anywhere south of Washington. The team on the ice was not at the calibre that would bring the fans flocking to the new stadium seats. They did have solid hockey talent like Gary Roberts and Sami Kapanen, but their defence had holes, and the goaltending was mediocre. The inaugural fanfare died down when they finished out of the playoffs and at the bottom of their division.

Raleigh, North Carolina's first taste of playoff hockey came in 1999, but the Boston Bruins dashed their hopes in the opening round. The Hurricanes lacked a few key players that would be needed to take them far into the post-season. It was during the 2001-02 that a real contending team began to take shape. The additions of rookies Erik Cole and Coach Peter Laviolette, and the clutch goaltending of Artus Irbe, brought them to the top of their division, and the team finally had hopes of making it past the first round.

In the first round, they faced off against the tough New Jersey Devils and their goaltender Martin Brodeur, but it was Irbe who proved to be the better goaltender leading his team to a 4-2 series victory. Carolina then dealt the Montréal Canadiens and the Toronto Maple Leafs early exits from the post-season. They had made it to the Stanley Cup finals, but their toughest challenge lay ahead, namely the Detroit Red Wings. The Hurricanes were no match for a team like Detroit, and the rookie coach learned a lesson in defeat from the master Wings coach Scotty Bowman.

The next two seasons were disasters. They finished both seasons in the basement of the league and out of the playoffs. It was almost as if the franchise needed the NHL lockout of the 2004-05 season to recuperate and get the team back on the winning track of 2002. With the new rule changes implemented during the lockout to improve the offence of the game, the Carolina Hurricanes that once held back and played boring defensive hockey now exploded offensively while never forgetting the solid defence.

Adding to their offensive power the Hurricanes activated young rookie sensation Eric Staal and saw it pay immediate dividends. Also coming out of their shells were Justin Williams, Erik Cole and another young rookie goaltender Cam Ward.

Staal finished his rookie season with 45 goals and 55 assist as the leading scorer on the team. His talents rubbed off on the other players as well, with Williams garnering 76 points overall and Cole potting 31 goals.

The Canes finished atop their division and entered into the playoffs with hopes of getting back into the Stanley Cup finals. Their first round opponents were the Montréal Canadiens. Even when the Hurricanes were known as the Hartford Whalers, they never got along with the Canadiens. Regular season games were always physical affairs, and the playoffs got downright nasty at times. The 2005 series against the Habs was no different. After two games, it appeared as if the Canadiens were going to come away with the upset series sweep taking the first two games in convincing fashion. But an injury to their captain Saku Koivu when Justin Williams' stick caught him in the eye, seemed to take the wind out of the Habs' sails. The Hurricanes came back to win the next four straight games to eliminate their rivals from the hunt for the Cup. After two sub-par performances in the opening two games, the Canes replaced veteran goaltender Martin Gerber with rookie Cam Ward. The freshman netminder stole the series away from the Canadiens almost single-handedly and was instrumental in helping them in a relatively easy round against the New Jersey Devils. The Canes would need seven games to defeat their conference final opponents, the Buffalo Sabres, but they came through victorious and had made it once again to the finals against the Edmonton Oilers.

For the first time in NHL history, two WHA franchises would play against each other in the finals. What followed was one of the most entertaining series in recent memory. The play was physical, the pace on the ice was feverish and the goaltending on both ends of the ice was spectacular.

The Hurricanes played physical and desperate in the first two games, and it paid off in a two game series lead. The Oilers appeared to be sitting back and letting the Hurricanes dictate the pace of the game, but not for long. Ryan Smith scored the game-winning goal in the third game to give the Oilers a 2-1 win and a foot up out of the playoff grave. Carolina pulled off a 2-1 victory in game four but allowed the Oilers to gain momentum after game five saw the Oilers win in dramatic fashion when Fernando Pisani grabbed the puck and broke in on Cam Ward for a shorthanded breakaway in overtime. The win reenergized the Oilers who trounced the Canes 4-0 in game six to send the series to the pivotal game seven. It was time for desperation hockey, and the Canes veterans led the way.

Rod Brind'Amour, Glen Wesley and Bret Hedican had all played 15 years in the league without winning a Cup, and their drive to end the streak inspired the other players on the team. The Oilers were no match in the final game, and the Hurricanes won the first Stanley Cup for the franchise. Captain Rod Brind'Amour received the Stanley Cup, and Cam Ward was awarded the Conn Smythe trophy for his incredible performance in goal.

First and Only Incredible Comeback

In the history of the league there have been incredible comebacks but nothing like the story of the Toronto Maple Leafs in the 1942 Stanley Cup finals.

At the end of the 1941-42 season, the New York Rangers were on top of the league with 60 points thanks to high-scoring forwards such as Bryan Hextall, Lynn Patrick and Phil Watson. Close behind in second place were the Maple Leafs who faced off against the high-scoring Rangers in the first round of the playoffs. All the sportswriters predicted an easy victory for the Rangers given their firepower and the fact that just two years earlier the almost exact same line-up had won the Stanley Cup. But as history has often proved, the pundits got it wrong, and the Leafs eliminated the Rangers in a convincing six games.

While the Leafs disposed of the Rangers, it was the Detroit Red Wings who came out of the preliminary rounds victorious and would go on to face Toronto after defeating the Montréal Canadiens and the Boston Bruins.

Toronto was delighted to have the Red Wings as their opponent. Detroit had finished the regular season with a losing record of 19-25 and seemed tired and worn out after two difficult series in the playoffs. All the papers in Toronto predicted an easy win for the Leafs, as did many in the dressing room before the start of game one. Detroit had some firepower in Don Grosso and Sid Abel, but the defence and goaltender Johnny Mowers had struggled throughout the season. The gambling types had Toronto as 8-5 favourites to take the series in convincing fashion. Aware of the gap between his team and the Maple Leafs, Detroit coach Jack Adams knew his team had one advantage over Toronto.

"We may not have the greatest hockey club in the world, but it's a club that's loaded with fighting heart," Adams proudly exclaimed. "If there's anything that wins hockey championships, it's just that."

The Red Wings came out fighting, just like their coach had promised and checked the Leafs into submission. The Leafs star line barely had time to touch the puck before a Red Wings player smashed them into the boards. Detroit's best forward Don Grosso put the Red Wings on the scoreboard just two minutes into the game. Toronto was obviously rattled by its opponent's strategy and could not mount a decent offence. Somehow they still managed to score two goals, but it wasn't enough, as Don Grosso put the game away in the third period with his second goal of the game. The score at the sound of the buzzer was 3-2, and the Leafs felt lucky to have kept the game so close.

After the game, Toronto coach Hap Day tried to explain what had happened. "There's nothing wrong with our club physically. It's a question whether or not we've got the stuff that champions are made of. That wasn't hockey out there—it was a fair display of hoodlumism, Detroit's stock in trade. But we've got to adjust ourselves to the Kitty-bar-the-door tactics if we're going to win the Cup."

In the Detroit dressing room, things were very different. While celebrating their victory, they were interrupted by several Detroit faithful, who had raised money from a group of fans who felt that their boys should be rewarded with some extra money after putting up such a fight to win the game.

Game two was no different. The Leafs could not mount any significant opposition to the Wingst heavy hitters and lost the game 4-2. Detroit was overflowing with confidence, while the Leafs were left searching for answers.

"We're still in the league, I guess," Adams mocked. "We out-fought them, out-hustled them and should have beat them 7-3."

Detroit power forward Sid Abel echoed the sentiments of confidence by stating: "Those Leafs will know they've had their hides blistered when they get through this series."

If Toronto did not beat the Red Wings in the third game, it would be almost impossible for them to come back from such a deficit. No other team had done it since the league had adopted the best-of-seven series, leaving Toronto with no example to draw from. The Leafs came out strong in game three and scored two quick goals from Lorne Carr in under a minute, but the celebrations did not last long as Detroit came back with two quick goals of their own to tie the game before the first period was finished. It got worse for Toronto in the second and third, as Detroit put the game away with three more unanswered goals to take the game 5-2. The Maple Leafs were at a loss to explain what was happening on the ice.

"Detroit is unbeatable," said Toronto goaltender Turk Broda, obviously frustrated at his team's inability to solve the Red Wings. "They're too hot, and they can't seem to do anything wrong."

Hap Day needed something to shake his team up if they were going to have any chance of winning one game at the very least. Day decided to bench veterans Bucko McDonald and Gord Drillion, who were having a good playoff series but weren't producing against the Red Wings' defensive system. Day replaced them with the fresh legs of Bob Goldham and Don Metz. All seemed to be going in the wrong direction, when at the midway point of the second period of game four, the Red Wings had taken the lead 2-0 and looked poised to sweep the series in front of the home crowd. All they had to do was hold the lead.

Toronto had other ideas, however, and quickly tied the game before the end of the second period. Detroit scored first in the third period, but Toronto got two more from Syl Apps and Nick Metz to take the game 4-3 and earn another shot at the series. Although the game was filled with action, the best was saved for the last two minutes. Frustrated at not being able to finish the game or just mad at the referee because of a perceived bias during the game, Red Wing Eddie Wares directed a volley of verbal assaults at referee Mel Harwood,

who promptly handed him a 10-minute miscon-
duct penalty. Just a short time later, Harwood
spotted Detroit with too many men on the ice
and whistled the play dead. When Don Grosso
was called out to serve the two-minute infraction,
he skated to the penalty box, stopped for a second
to think about his next move and skated over to
Harwood, dropping his stick and gloves in front
of the referee in disgust. When the final buzzer
sounded, all hell broke lose. Steaming mad at the
sudden turn of events, Detroit coach Jack Adams
jumped onto the ice and headed straight for
Harwood, who was settling the final game stats
in the penalty box, and pounced on the unsus-
pecting referee. While Harwood and the portly
Adams traded haymakers, Detroit fans took it
upon themselves to attack the linesmen. They
nearly got to league president Frank Calder, but
a group of policemen whisked him away before
the mob had a chance to vent their anger. After
everything was cleared up and cooler heads
reviewed the situation, Adams was fined and suspended indefinitely. Adams, in his oh-so-colourful
manner, refused to be held back.

"They can't keep me out of Maple Leaf Gardens.
I'll buy my way into the place," he said defiantly.

Game five was the turning point in the series.
Detroit tried to beat the Maple Leafs into submission

as in the previous games, but Toronto simply out-skated them on every level and finished the game with a 9-3 victory and a renewed sense that they could actually win the Cup.

After a penalty-laden game five, game six was extremely tame without one penalty called during the whole game. Detroit was playing Toronto's style of game now and lost 3-0 after a brilliant performance by Leafs goalie Turk Broda, who turned aside all 32 Red Wing shots, setting the stage for game seven.

Some 16,218 fans jammed into Maple Leaf Gardens on April 18, hoping to see the Leafs mark their place in the history books and win the Stanley Cup after coming back from a 3-0 series deficit. Over the roar of the crowd, the first whistle could barely be heard as the referee dropped the puck for the opening face-off. The Leafs fans quickly fell silent, when at the 1:44 mark of the second period, Detroit's Syd Howe scored to put the Wings in the lead. Nervous tension built up in the arena as the rest of the second period went by without a goal from the Leafs, but the crowd erupted to life again in the third period when Sweeney Schriner tipped in a shot from the point to tie the game. Toronto took the lead with a goal by Pete Langelle and sealed Detroit's fate on the second goal of the game from Schriner.

As the clock slowly ran down, Jack Adams bitterly accepted his fate. "Hap did a great job. Toronto deserved to win, I guess," added Adams. "But I think they were a little bit lucky."

As the buzzer sounded, the Maple Leafs piled onto the ice and graciously shook hands with the Red Wing players. It had been a tough series, one in which both teams were left with an equal number of cuts and bruises, but only Toronto was able to hold Lord Stanley's Cup high above their heads. They went down into the record books as the only champions ever to come back from a 3-0 series deficit to win the Cup.

First Canada Cup

After the excitement generated by the 1972 Summit Series and to a lesser extent the 1974 Series (funny how our history seems to have removed from the collective consciousness that the Soviets beat up on our Canadians players in 1974 with four decisive victories—one loss and three ties), interest in world professional hockey spiked. It seemed that the Olympics were not enough to quench hockey fans' desire to crown the nation that would hold the bragging rights at having the best hockey players in the world. At that time it was only a team of amateurs that a country could send to compete in the Olympics. So when people got to see their very best face-off, it created a need for a new tournament. In 1976, Czechoslovakia, Canada, Sweden, Finland, The Soviet Union, the United States and (in 1984 only) West Germany, competed in the first Canada Cup.

The Canadian team was stacked with the best NHL players at the time. Bobby Orr, Denis Potvin, Bobby Hull, Gilbert Perreault, Phil Esposito and goaltender Rogie Vachon made their appearance for Canada and showed the other countries that they were in for a difficult task by beating the poor Finns 11-2. The only team to provide any challenge was the Czechoslovakian team who beat them in a close a game by a final score of 1-0.

Canada cruised through games with the U.S.A. (CAN 4, U.S.A. 2) Sweden (CAN 4, SWE 0) and the USSR (CAN 3, USSR 1) to face Czechoslovakia in the final best-of-three series.

Canada's Bobby Orr, playing on bad knees that pained him through the entire tournament and that later forced him to retire, had the tournament of a lifetime, scoring twice and assisting on seven goals. He was the leader of the team providing the inspiration for the Canadian squad to win the tournament with a 6-0 win in game one and a 5-4 (OT) win to take the first Canada Cup tournament.

Until 1991, Canada won all Canada Cup tournaments, four in total, except one that was taken from them by the Soviet Union in 1981. In 1996, the tournament was later renamed the World Cup of Hockey.

Chapter Seven

Quick Hits

First Time the Stanley Cup Took a Shower

It is a tradition that after a team wins the Stanley Cup, each player from the team gets the trophy for the day to do pretty much whatever they want with it. Many players take the Cup back to their hometowns to family picnics and barbecues, but not many have taken the Cup into the shower. Except for Steve Yzerman, that is.

Not wanting to be apart from the Cup for a single moment Steve Yzerman had a dilemma on his hands when he needed to take a shower, but rather than leave the Cup just outside the bathroom door, Yzerman introduced Lord Stanley to a new level of intimacy by taking a shower with the Cup. Others players have taken that intimacy to whole other levels.

First, and Not the Last, Time the Cup Was Not Used Properly

It is tradition that after a team wins the Stanley Cup that players take turns drinking champagne from the bowl, but in the Cup's long history there have been many other substances that have found their way into bowl that would make one think twice before ever letting it touch your lips.

The first horrifying story comes after the Detroit Red Wings won the Stanley Cup in 1937. During the celebrations, after consuming copious amounts of alcohol, Red Wings forward Gord Pettinger mistook the legendary trophy for a bowl of the porcelain kind and promptly filled it with urine.

Many fans and players refer to the Stanley Cup as the Holy Grail of hockey and consider any defilement as a sacrilege that risks a curse being placed on the player or team. The New York Rangers were made firm believers in the curse after winning the 1940 Stanley Cup Championship.

Not only did the entire New York Rangers team use the Cup as their personal toilet, but Rangers president John Kilpatrick also burned the deed to the fully paid mortgage on Madison Square Garden in the bowl of the Cup. The hockey gods did not ignore these two desecrations of the sacred Stanley Cup. Legend goes that a curse was placed on the team. That curse would last

54 years until the Stanley Cup once again graced the halls of Madison Square Garden.

Whether they're believers or not, most professional players will not leave anything to chance and dare to mess with the hockey gods. However, that is not the worst thing to have found its way into the Stanley Cup. The ultimate sacrilege came from an innocent child.

Just moments after winning the Stanley Cup in 1964, the Toronto Maple Leafs Red Kelly was forced to leave the celebrations to catch a train to Ottawa to attend to more pressing matters as an Honourable Member of Parliament representing the liberal party and the good people of York West, Ottawa. Because of his extracurricular activities, Kelly never got a chance to have his photo taken with the Cup, so Leafs owner Harold Ballard, being the nice guy he is so well known to be, had the Cup and a photographer sent to the Kelly household for a photo session.

The entire Kelly family gathered for the photo session in the living room, even Kelly's infant son. Thinking it would make a really cute picture, Kelly placed his naked infant son in the bowl of the cup for the shot. The picture was a wonderful memory, but his son left behind some memories of his own.

"He did the whole load in the Cup. He did every-thing," said Kelly in a later interview. "That's why our family always laughs when we see players drinking champagne from the Cup."

Would you still take that drink?

The First Woman on the Stanley Cup

Marguerite Norris and her family purchased the Detroit Red Wings in 1932, and when her father James Norris Sr. passed away in 1952, con-trol of the team passed into her hands. That also happened to be the year the Red Wings won eight straight playoff games to take home the Stanley Cup, and since Marguerite Norris was the presi-dent of the team, she became the first ever woman to have her name engraved on the Stanley Cup. Seven other women have since had their names engraved on the Stanley Cup:

- Sonia Scurfield (1989), a co-owner of the Calgary Flames

- Marie-Denise DeBartolo York (1991), presi-dent of the Pittsburgh Penguins

- Marian Ilitch (1997, 1998), a co-owner of the Detroit Red Wings

- Denise Ilitch (1997, 1998), vice president of the Detroit Red Wings

- Lisa Ilitch (1997, 1998), vice president of the Detroit Red Wings

- Carole Ilitch Trepeck (1997, 1998), vice president of the Detroit Red Wings

- Charlotte Grahame, Director of Hockey Administration, was added in 2001 when Colorado won the Cup

First Use of a Helmet

Playing for the Boston Bruins in 1929, George Owen briefly wore a leather football helmet when he was a rookie defenceman in the league. Despite the funny looks he got, Owen helped his team on to the Stanley Cup championship that year.

First Use of Names on the Jerseys

In order to make the game easier for an American audience not used to the game of hockey, the New York Americans were the first team to put player names on jerseys during the 1925-26 NHL season. The National Hockey League did not make names on jerseys mandatory until 1978.

The First Marsh Peg

For over 40 years, Fred Marsh worked in arenas at every level of operation. He had always dreamed of making it into the NHL, but when he realized he didn't have the talent he wanted he still wished to remain close to the game he loved.

Fred loved everything about the game, and he was always seeking new ways to help improve the game. One of his biggest concerns was that many players were suffering injuries and having their careers ended prematurely because of the immovable hockey nets. When you take a speeding hockey player and combine that with stationary metal posts, injuries are bound to happen. Fred Marsh had the solution.

Marsh came up with a simple, yet ingenious solution: flexible pegs. Normally, the nets were anchored solidly into the ice. With the patented Marsh Pegs, the nets stand up to game time abuse, but if a player crashes into the net, the net simply lifts up out of the hole and the referee whistles the play dead.

Marsh Pegs are now standard issue in the NHL and in most rinks and arenas around the world. Fred Marsh made it into the NHL after all.

First Official Use of the Hockey Net

While it is possible that any enterprising hockey player might have thrown a net over the standard posts that marked the goal line, a report in a Halifax newspaper on January 6, 1899, officially mentions the use of a net in a game between two clubs from the Halifax region. The Canadian Hockey

League adopted a similar design before the start of the 1899-1900 season.

First Player to Score a Playoff Hat Trick with Two Teams

On May 17, 1981, New York Islander legend Butch Goring scored three goals in a 7-5 beating delivered to the Minnesota North Stars in game three of the Stanley Cup finals. The Islanders then went on to defeat the Stars and win their second straight Stanley Cup. Goring had previously scored a hat trick as a member of the Los Angeles Kings in the 1976–77 playoffs against the Boston Bruins. Goring did not win the Cup that year.

Shutout Streak

On December 27, 1919, the Ottawa Senators became the first NHL team to begin a season with two straight shutouts in a 2-0 win over the Montréal Canadiens. The other win came against the Québec Bulldogs. The goaltender for Ottawa in both games was the legendary Clint Benedict.

The First of the Trophy Winners

Stanley Cup	1893 Montréal Amateur Athletic Association
Art Ross Trophy	1918 Joe Malone, Montréal Canadiens
Calder Trophy	1933 Carl Voss, Detroit Red Wings

Hart Trophy	1924 Frank Nighbor, Ottawa Senators
Jack Adams Trophy	1974 Fred Shero, Philadelphia Flyers
Conn Smythe Trophy	1965 Jean Béliveau, Montréal Canadiens
Norris Trophy	1954 Red Kelly, Detroit Red Wings
Presidents Trophy (Official)	1986 Edmonton Oilers
Frank Selke Trophy	1978 Bob Gainey, Montréal Canadiens
Vezina Trophy	1927 George Hainsworth, Montréal Canadiens
Maurice Richard Trophy	1999 Teemu Selanne, Mighty Ducks of Anaheim

Fast Firsts

January 12, 1918: The Ottawa Senators' Dave Ritchie became the first player in the National Hockey League to score a goal with two teams in one season when he scored a goal in a 9-4 loss against the Montréal Canadiens. He began the season with the Montréal Wanderers, scoring five goals with that club before the club folded and he was moved to Ottawa.

January 12, 1918: Montréal Canadiens superstar "The Phantom" Joe Malone scored five times in that same game against Ottawa to become the first person in NHL history to reach the 20-goal plateau in a season.

February 19, 1918: Montréal Canadiens goaltender Georges Vezina recorded the first NHL shutout in a 9-0 victory of the Toronto Arenas.

March 20, 1918: The Toronto Arenas became the first NHL team to compete for the Stanley Cup when they faced off against the Pacific Coast Hockey Association champs the Vancouver Millionaires.

March 30, 1918: The Toronto Arenas became the first NHL Stanley Cup winners when they beat the Vancouver Millionaires 2-1 in the final game of a best-of-five series.

December 28, 1918: Canadiens goaltending legend Georges Vezina became the first NHL goalie to record an assist in a 6-3 victory over Toronto.

February 12, 1919: Ottawa Senators goaltender Clint Benedict became the first goaltender to record two shutouts in one season with a 7-0 victory over the Montréal Canadiens.

March 19, 1919: Harry "Hap" Holmes of the Seattle Metropolitans became the first goaltender to record a shutout in a Stanley Cup playoff series, against the Montréal Canadiens.

March 22, 1919: Montréal Canadiens star Newsy Lalonde became the first player to score four goals in a Stanley Cup finals game, leading the Canadiens to a 4-2 victory over the Seattle Metropolitans in game two of the series.

April 1, 1919: An outbreak of the Spanish Influenza resulted in the first time a Stanley Cup championship was cancelled.

December 27, 1919: The Ottawa Senators became the first team to open a season with two straight shutouts with a 2-0 victory over the Montréal Canadiens.

January 31, 1920: The Québec Bulldog's Joe Malone was the first and only player to score seven goals in one NHL game. He helped his team to a 10-6 victory over Toronto.

March 24, 1920: The Ottawa Senators' goaltender Clint Benedict recorded his first career playoff shutout with a 3-0 win over the Seattle Metropolitans in game two of the Stanley Cup finals. In total Benedict recorded 15 career playoff shutouts—a record that wasn't broken until Patrick Roy came along in 2001.

December 22, 1920: The Hamilton Tigers became the first and only team to record a shutout in its NHL debut when the Tigers beat the Montréal Canadiens 5-0.

March 10, 1921: The Ottawa Senators George Boucher became the first NHL defenceman to score a playoff hat trick when his Senators beat Toronto 5-0.

March 21, 1921: Eleven thousand fans, the largest crowd ever to watch a hockey game, packed into a Vancouver arena to watch the home team Millionaires win game one of the Stanley Cup finals 3-1 over the Ottawa Senators.

April 4, 1921: The Ottawa Senators defeated the Vancouver Millionaires to become the first NHL team to win consecutive Stanley Cup Championships.

January 14, 1922: Brothers Odie and Sprague Cleghorn became the first family members to score four goals apiece in one game as they led their Montréal Canadiens to a 10-6 victory over the Hamilton Tigers.

February 11, 1922: After three periods of play, the Toronto St. Pats and the Ottawa Senators went into overtime. Neither team could score in the 20-minute overtime period, and they had to settle for a 4-4 tie. It was the first NHL game that ended in a tie.

January 31, 1923: The Montréal Canadiens beat the Hamilton Tigers 5-4 in the National Hockey League's first penalty-free game.

March 23, 1923: Foster Hewitt broadcasts his first game.

March 31, 1923: An 18-year-old King Clancy became the first and only NHL player to play all six positions on the ice in one game when his Senators beat the Edmonton Eskimos in game two of the Stanley Cup finals. In those days, when a goaltender received a penalty they had to serve the time in the box themselves. When Ottawa goaltender Clint Benedict got a penalty, King Clancy stepped in to guard his net for two minutes.

March 25, 1924: The Montréal Canadiens won their first Stanley Cup after the formation of the NHL in 1917. The team's first Stanley Cup came when they were part of the National Hockey Association in 1916.

March 1924: The Ottawa Senators' Frank Nighbor was awarded the NHL's first individual trophy when he was given the Hart Trophy as the league MVP.

November 29, 1924: The Montréal Forum officially opened its doors for business when the hockey shrine hosted the Canadiens and the Toronto St. Patricks. The Canadiens won the game 7-1.

December 17, 1924: Goaltender Jake Forbes of the Hamilton Tigers and Alex Connell of the Ottawa Senators played to the first 0-0 tie in NHL history.

January 20, 1925: Clint Benedict became the first goaltender to record 20 career shutouts when his Montréal Maroons beat the Boston Bruins 2-0.

March 4, 1925: Ottawa Senator Cy Denneny became the first player in NHL history to record 200 career goals when he scored one in a 5-1 victory over the Montréal Canadiens.

March 30, 1925: The Western Hockey League's Victoria Cougars became the last non-NHL team to win the Stanley Cup when they beat Montréal 6-1 in the final game of a best-of-five series.

December 15, 1925: The Montréal Canadiens beat the New York Americans at Madison Square Garden. It was the first NHL game played in New York City.

March 4, 1926: Nels Stewart of the Montréal Maroons became the first rookie to lead the NHL in scoring, finishing the season with 42 points.

March 16, 1926: Ottawa Senators goaltender Alex Connell became the first goaltender to record 15 shutouts in one season with a 4-0 win over the Toronto St. Pats.

March 19, 1927: Montréal Canadiens became the first team to shut out the same opponent four straight times. The unlucky team was the rival Montréal Maroons.

March 26, 1927: Ottawa Senators goaltender Alex Connell became the first goalie to win 30 games in a season with a 3-2 win over the Canadiens.

March 31, 1927: The Canadiens' Howie Morenz scored the winning goal in the first-ever playoff overtime game. His Canadiens beat the Maroons 1-0.

March 22, 1928: Ottawa Senators Alex Connell became the first goaltender to record 50 career shutouts with a 5-0 victory over the New York Americans.

March 24, 1928: The Canadiens' Howie Morenz became the first player in NHL history to record 50 points in one season.

March 2, 1929: George Hainsworth became the first goaltender in NHL history to record 20 shutouts in one season with a 3-0 victory over the Boston Bruins.

January 21, 1930: The Boston Bruins became the first team in NHL history to score 100 goals in a season in a 5-1 win over the Chicago Black Hawks. Cooney Weiland scored the actual goal.

February 20, 1930: Montréal Maroons Clint Benedict became the first NHL goaltender to wear a mask in game in a 3-3 tie against the New York Americans.

November 22, 1930: The Toronto Maple Leafs became the first team in NHL history to open the season with five straight shutouts with a 2-0 win over the Ottawa Senators.

January 3, 1931: Nels Stewart of the Montréal Maroons became the first and only player to score 2 goals four seconds apart in a 5-3 victory over the Bruins.

February 14, 1931: When the Toronto Maple Leafs' Charlie Conacher scored against the Detroit Red Wings, it was the first time in NHL history that three assists were awarded. The recipients were King Clancy, Joe Primeau and Busher Jackson.

April 5, 1932: The Toronto Maple Leafs' Busher Jackson became the first player to record a play-off hat trick in one period. He accomplished this feat in the second period of a 6-4 win over the New York Rangers in game one of the Stanley Cup finals.

September 30, 1933: The NHL used two referees this season instead of the one to officiate the games.

March 12, 1933: John Ross Roach became the first goaltender in NHL history to record 200 career wins in a 3-1 Detroit Red Wings win over the Canadiens.

January 16, 1934: Ken Doraty of the Toronto Maple Leafs scored the only overtime hat trick in NHL history in a 7-4 win over Ottawa. Overtime was a 10-minute period in those days and not sudden death.

November 13, 1934: St. Louis Eagles Ralph Bowman scored the first penalty shot goal during a 2-1 loss to the Montréal Maroons.

March 22, 1936: For the first time in NHL history, all the teams in one division finished the season with records above .500. Detroit, Boston, Chicago and New York were part of the American Division.

September 24, 1937: For the first time, the NHL adopted the "icing rule."

December 21, 1937: Chicago's Paul Thompson became the first player to score a goal against his brother, when he scored on the Boston Bruins' Cecil Thompson in a 2-1 loss.

March 17, 1938: Nels Stewart became the first player to score 300 career goals.

March 1938: The Detroit Red Wings became the first team to miss the playoffs one year after winning the Stanley Cup.

April 6, 1939: The Boston Bruins and the Toronto Maple Leafs played in the first best-of-seven series in a Stanley Cup final.

February 25, 1940: The New York Rangers faced the Montréal Canadiens in the first hockey game televised in the United States.

March 17, 1940: For the first time one line—Milt Schmidt, Woody Dumart and Bobby Bauer—finished first, second and third in scoring.

November 12, 1942: Sixteen-year-old Armand Guidolin became the youngest player in NHL history when he played his first game for the Boston Bruins.

January 3, 1943: Chicago's Reg Bently scored and was assisted by his brothers Max and Doug in a 3-3 tie with the Rangers. This was the first NHL goal with three points all from the same family.

January 14, 1943: Montréal Canadiens Alex Smart became the first rookie to score a hat trick in his first NHL game.

March 25, 1943: The Bruins' Harvey Jackson scored the first shorthanded overtime goal in playoff history as his Bruins defeated the Montréal Canadiens 3-2 in game three of the Stanley Cup semi-finals.

December 19, 1943: Harry Lumley became the youngest goaltender in NHL history when, playing for the Detroit Red Wings, he debuted in a 6-2 loss to the Rangers. He was 17 years old.

February 20, 1944: The Chicago Black Hawks and the Toronto Maple Leafs played in the only penalty-free, scoreless game in NHL history.

March 18, 1944: The Montréal Canadiens became the first team to go undefeated at home for an entire season with a final 11-2 victory over the New York Rangers.

February 25, 1945: Montréal's Maurice Richard set an NHL record by scoring his 45th goal of the season. He beat out previous record holder Joe Malone's 44-goal season in 1917-18.

March 17, 1945: The Detroit Red Wings Bill Hollett became the first defenceman to score 20 goals in a season in a 4-3 win over Toronto.

March 18, 1945: Maurice Richard became the first player to score 50 goals in one season after a 4-2 Canadiens victory over the Bruins.

October 16, 1946: Detroit's Gordie Howe played in his first NHL game and scored his first career goal in a 3-3 tie with Toronto. He also got into two fights.

November 13, 1947: The NHL began a policy for the first time to allow players to raise their sticks up in the air to signify a goal. The Canadiens Billy Reay became the first when Montréal beat Chicago 5-2 at the Forum.

April 16, 1949: The Toronto Maple Leafs became the first NHL team to win three straight Stanley Cups when they defeated the Detroit Red Wings in four straight games.

February 5, 1950: Dick Irvin became the first coach in NHL history to record 500 wins when his Canadiens defeated the Bruins 5-3 at the Montréal Forum.

April 23, 1950: The first game seven overtime in Stanley Cup history was played, and Pete Badando of the Detroit Red Wings scored the 4-3 winner over the Rangers to win the Cup. Overtime heroics were born.

March 15, 1951: The Detroit Red Wings became the first NHL team to win 40 games in one season with a 4-0 victory over the Bruins.

April 21, 1951: Bill Barilko scored the Stanley Cup–winning goal in the fifth game of the Stanley Cup finals against Montréal. It was the only series in NHL history in which every game went into overtime.

November 21, 1951: Chicago Black Hawks 46-year-old trainer Moe Roberts was sent in to play in goal to replace an injured Harry Lumley. Roberts helped defeat the Red Wings 6-2.

March 23, 1952: In a 7–6 victory over the Rangers, Chicago Black Hawks Bill Mosienko scored three goals in 21 seconds.

November 1, 1952: Hockey was televised for the first time nationally in Canada from the Maple Leaf Gardens on the CBC, as the Leafs beat the Bruins 3-2.

January 29, 1953: Maurice Richard became the first player to score 20 or more goals in his first 10 full seasons in the NHL.

March 21, 1954: Gordie Howe became the first player to lead the league in scoring for four straight seasons.

December 18, 1954: Maurice Richard became the first player in NHL history to score 400 career goals when the Canadiens defeated the Black Hawks 4-2.

March 17, 1955: Montréal fans incite the first riot over a hockey player when Maurice Richard is suspended for the remainder of the season and the playoffs.

October 6, 1955: Detroit goaltender Glenn Hall played the first game of his incredible 502-complete-game streak in a 3-2 loss to the Black Hawks. Seven years later the streak ended.

December 29, 1955: For the first time, NHL officials wore new vertical stripped black and white sweaters in a game between Montréal and Toronto.

February 11, 1957: The NHL Players Association was formed, and Detroit's Ted Lindsay was named its first president.

October 19, 1957: Maurice Richard became the first player in NHL history to score 500 career goals as the Canadiens beat the Black Hawks 3-1.

January 18, 1958: Willie O'Ree played his first game for the Bruins becoming the first black player to play in the NHL.

April 18, 1959: Montréal became the first team to win four consecutive Stanley Cups with a finals series win over the Toronto Maple Leafs.

November 1, 1959: The Canadiens' Jacques Plante returned to the ice wearing a mask after being hit in the face with a puck.

April 14, 1960: Montréal became the only team to win the Stanley Cup five consecutive times.

November 27, 1960: Gordie Howe of the Red Wings became the first player to record 1000 career points in a 2-0 win over the Toronto Maple Leafs.

August 26, 1961: The Hockey Hall of Fame opened for the first time.

November 26, 1961: Gordie Howe became the first player to play in 1000 career regular season games in a 4-1 Red Wings loss to Chicago.

November 4, 1962: Detroit Red Wings Bill Gadsby became the first defenceman to score 500 career points in a 3-1 win over the Black Hawks.

June 5, 1963: NHL held its first Amateur Draft in Montréal. The first player selected was Garry Monahan.

November 8, 1963: Maple Leafs Gardens became the first arena to install separate penalty box doors for each team.

November 21, 1964: The Maple Leafs' Terry Sawchuk became the first goaltender to record a shutout in 16 straight seasons with a 1-0 win over Chicago.

January 27, 1965: Ulf Sterner became the first Swedish-born player to make it to the NHL.

He played his first game with the Rangers in a 5-2 victory over the Bruins.

May 1, 1965: Montréal's Jean Béliveau became the first winner of the Conn Smythe Trophy, given to the playoff MVP.

March 12, 1966: Bobby Hull of the Black Hawks became the first player in NHL history to score more than 50 goals in one season when he potted his 51st in a 4-2 win over the Rangers. He would finish the season with 54.

March 4, 1967: Terry Sawchuk became the first goaltender to record 100 shutouts when his Leafs beat Chicago 3-0.

April 9, 1968: Minnesota North Star Wayne Connelly became the first player in NHL history to score a penalty shot goal in the playoffs when he beat Los Angeles Kings goalie Terry Sawchuk.

May 10, 1968: Boston's Bobby Orr was named winner of the Norris Trophy (given to the best defenceman) for the first of a record eight consecutive seasons.

March 2, 1969: Phil Esposito of the Bruins scored twice to become the first player in NHL history to score 100 points in a season in a 4-0 victory over the Penguins.

January 3, 1970: Gordie Howe and George Armstrong became the first players in the NHL to play in four different decades.

April 5, 1970: Bobby Orr finished the season with 120 points to lead the NHL in scoring. He was the first defenceman to do so.

October 29, 1970: Gordie Howe became the first player in NHL history to record 1000 career points.

March 20, 1971: Ken Dryden and Dave Dryden made NHL history as the first two brothers to play against each other in a game. Ken's Canadiens beat Dave's Sabres 5-2.

October 31, 1971: Fred Glover became the first coach in NHL history to coach two teams in one season. He coached the Los Angeles Kings and the Oakland Seals.

March 12, 1974: Boston Bruin Bobby Orr became the first player to score 100 points in five straight seasons.

October 8, 1975: Doug Jarvis of the Montréal Canadiens played his first of a record 964 consecutive games.

February 7, 1976: Darryl Sittler of the Maple Leafs was the first to record 10 points in one game (six goals and four assists), against the Boston Bruins.

April 3, 1977: The Montréal Canadiens became the first team to win 60 games in one season with a 2-1 victory over the Washington Capitals.

April 1, 1978: Mike Bossy of the New York Islanders became the first NHL rookie to score 50 goals in a season in a 3-2 win over the Capitals.

November 28, 1979: Billy Smith of the New York Islanders became the first goalie to be credited for scoring a goal—he was the last Islander to touch the puck before the Colorado Rockies accidentally scored on their own empty net.

January 2, 1980: Gordie Howe became the first player in NHL history to appear in five different decades when he played for the Hartford Whalers in a 3-3 tie against the Oilers.

February 11, 1982: Referee Kerry Fraser became the first official to award two penalty shots in the same period.

March 25, 1982: Wayne Gretzky of the Edmonton Oilers scored two goals and two assists against the Calgary Flames to become the first player in NHL history to score 200 points in a season.

March 28, 1982: The Edmonton Oilers' Wayne Gretzky became the first player to score 90 goals in a season.

September 9, 1982: Washington coach Bryan Murray named his younger brother as assistant, becoming the first brother coaching team in NHL history.

November 19, 1983: Bruce Hood became the first referee to officiate 1000 NHL games when Toronto beat Detroit.

October 11, 1984: On his first shot on his first shift, Pittsburgh's Mario Lemieux scored his first NHL goal.

April 6, 1985: Pittsburgh Penguins became the first team to lose 50 or more games in three straight years when they lost 7-4 to the Capitals.

April 4, 1987: Denis Potvin of the New York Islanders became the first defenceman in NHL history to score 1000 career points.

May 19, 1989: Montréal's Larry Robinson became the first player in NHL history to play in 200 career playoff games.

October 26, 1990: Wayne Gretzky became the first player in NHL history to score 2000 points with an assist in an LA Kings win over the Winnipeg Jets.

October 17, 1992: Los Angeles Kings right-winger Jari Kurri became the first European-trained player to score 500 goals, in an 8-6 win over the Bruins.

October 6, 1993: Roger Neilson became the first NHL coach to lead six different NHL teams when he took the helm as the Florida Panthers head coach.

March 25, 1995: Detroit Red Wings Scotty Bowman became the first coach in NHL history to win 900 games.

May 3, 1995: In a lockout-shortened season, Pittsburgh's Jaromir Jagr became the first European player to lead the NHL in scoring.

October 3, 1997: The Vancouver Canucks and the Mighty Ducks of Anaheim faced-off at Tokyo's Yoyogi Arena, in the first NHL game played outside North America. The Canucks won 3-2.

April 23, 2002: Patrick Roy became the first goaltender to record 20 shutouts as the Avalanche beat the Kings 1-0.

June 5, 2006: In game one of the Stanley Cup Finals against the Carolina Hurricanes, Chris Pronger of the Edmonton Oilers became the first player in NHL history to score a penalty shot goal in a Stanley Cup Final game.

Notes on Sources

Black, Rod. *Lillehammer '94: Canada's Olympic Stories.* Toronto: Infact Publishing, 1994.

Judd, Ron C. *The Winter Olympics.* Seattle: The Mountaineers Books, 2008.

Edit. Macleans. *Canada Our Century in Sport.* Markham: Fitzhenry & Whiteside, 2002.

MacGregor, Roy. *A Loonie for Luck.* Toronto: McClelland & Stewart, 2002.

Podnieks, Andrew. *Canada's Olymspic Hockey Teams.* Toronto: Doubleday Canada LTD, 1997.

Wallechinsky, David and Jaime Loucky. *The Complete Book of the Winter Olympics.* Toronto: Sports Media Publishing, 2005.

Web Sources

CTV (n.d) http://www.ctvolympics.ca/ (accessed April 15 to May 20, 2009).

http://www.databaseolympics.com/ (accessed from April15 to May 20, 2009).

Canadian Broadcasting Corporation (n.d) http://www. cbc.ca/news/story/2007/02/12/vancouver-countdown. html, http://www.cbc.ca/canada/british-columbia/ story/2009/05/18/bc-sex-worker-training.html, http:// www.cbc.ca/canada/british-columbia/story/2007/05/08/ bc-atlanta.html, http://www.cbc.ca/sports/hockey/ story/2008/10/17/steve-yzerman.html, (accessed from April 15 to May 20, 2009).

Hockey Canada (n.d) http://www.hockeycanada.ca/ index.php/ci_id/57519/la_id/1.htm (accessed from April 15 to May 20, 2009).

Skate Canada (n.d) http://www.skatecanada.ca/en/ about_skate_canada/history/, http://www.skatecanada. ca/en/news_views/press_room/news_releases/2009/? CFID=9996792&CFTOKEN=55118222, (accessed from April 15 to May 20, 2009).

Freestyle Ski Canada (n.d) http://www.freestyleski.ca/ en/archives/, (accessed from April 15 to May 20, 2009).

Canski (n.d.) http://www.canski.org/webconcepteur/ web/alpine, (accessed from April 15 to May 20, 2009).

J. Alexander Poulton

J. Alexander Poulton is a writer, photographer and genuine enthusiast of Canada's national pastime. A resident of Montréal all his life, he has developed a healthy passion for hockey ever since he saw his first Montréal Canadiens game. His favorite memory was meeting the legendary gentleman hockey player Jean Beliveau, who in 1988 towered over the young awestruck author.

He earned his B.A. in English Literature from McGill University and his graduate diploma in Journalism from Concordia University. He has 13 other books to his credit, including *Canadian Hockey Record Breakers, Greatest Games of the Stanley Cup, Greatest Moments in Canadian Hockey, Canadian Hockey Trivia, Hockey's Hottest Defensemen, The Montréal Canadiens, The Toronto Maple Leafs* and his most recent offering *Does This Make Me Look Fat? Canadian Sports Humour.*

OverTime Books

If you enjoyed *Hockey Firsts*, be sure to check out these other great titles from OverTime Books:

New!
WEIRD FACTS ABOUT GOLF: Strange, Wacky & Hilarious Stories
by Stephen Drake

Most golf historians agree that the game was invented in Scotland more than 500 years ago, but the Chinese claim to have invented a game that involved hitting a ball with a stick towards a target as far back as 943 AD. Nowadays, one can play a round on the ice floes of the Arctic, on the plains of Africa and in the war zones of Afghanistan and Iraq. The rich history of the sport has produced a wealth of screwball, outlandish and weird tales.

Softcover • 5.25" X 8.25" • 224 pages • ISBN13 978-1-897277-25-6 • $14.95

New!
WEIRD FACTS ABOUT BASEBALL: Strange, Wacky & Hilarious Stories
by J. Alexander Poulton

When people think of baseball, they often picture a sport of grace, class and poetic athleticism, but in reality baseball is equally a game of errors, bloopers and crazy moments. *Weird Facts About Baseball* is a collection of the most ridiculous, funny and wacky moments that have happened in the history of the game. From a pitcher biting his own bum with his false teeth to a catcher falling asleep at the plate during a game, this book has it all! If you appreciate the lighter side of sports then you will certainly love *Weird Facts About Baseball*.

Softcover • 5.25" X 8.25" • 224 pages • ISBN13 978-1-897277-28-7 • $14.95

SIDNEY CROSBY
by J. Alexander Poulton

This biography features stories from Sidney Crosby's first steps on the ice to his leadership of the Pittsburgh Penguins in the Stanley Cup playoffs.

Softcover • 5.25" X 8.25" • 176 pages • ISBN13 978-1-897277-20-1 • $9.95

WEIRD FACTS ABOUT CURLING: Strange, Wacky, Informative & Hilarious
by Geoffrey Lansdell, with contributions by Carla MacKay

Scottish immigrants brought the game "across the pond" in the 18th century. Since then, the roaring game has amassed its fair share of amusing and interesting stories, facts and anecdotes. Read about curling's on-again, off-again status with the Olympic games, flamboyant characters like "Pizza Paul" Gowsell and much more.

Softcover • 5.25" X 8.25" • 256 pages • ISBN13 978-1-897277-30-0 • $18.95

HOCKEY QUOTES
compiled by J. Alexander Poulton

This book is a collection of some of the greatest, funniest and most memorable words spoken when hockey heroes swap game day for wordplay. Witty, insightful and just plain confusing quotations about coaching, hockey hair, attitude, penalties and much more.

Softcover • 5.25" X 8.25" • 168 pages • ISBN13 978-1-897277-35-5 • $9.95

Lone Pine Publishing is the exclusive distributor for OverTime Books.
If you cannot find these titles at your local bookstore, contact us:
Canada: 1-800-661-9017 USA: 1-800-518-3541